DATE DUE

What Works with Children

We would like to thank the talented children who gave us permission to use their artwork in this volume:
Alex K., Alex R., Carden, Carolina, Casey, Dana, Danielle, Elizabeth, Erin, Ethan, Frances,
Hannah, John, Katie, Kerry, Kylie, Laura, Lauren, Lindsay, Morgan, Nelson, Trevis, and Zac.

The editors and authors
of this book
are proud to donate
their royalties to

 **Save the
Children**

SAVE THE CHILDREN

is an international relief and developmental

organization dedicated to making lasting,

positive change in the lives of children in

need in the United States and forty-six

countries around the world.

What Works with Children

WISDOM & REFLECTIONS

FROM PEOPLE WHO HAVE DEVOTED THEIR CAREERS TO KIDS

Edited by Marshall P. Duke
& Sara Bookman Duke

PEACHTREE
ATLANTA

Dedication

To our grandmothers—
Anna Bookman and Helen Cherry.
Your stories live on.

Published by
PEACHTREE PUBLISHERS, LTD.
1700 Chattahoochee Avenue
Atlanta, Georgia 30318-2112

www.peachtree-online.com

Text © 2000 by Marshall P. Duke and Sara Bookman Duke, and the respective authors of each essay.
Cover illustrations and interior illustrations © 2000 by the respective artists.

Cover and book design by Loraine M. Balcsik

Manufactured in the United States of America

10 9 8 7 6 5 4 3 2

Library of Congress Cataloging-in-Publication Data

What works with children : wisdom and reflections from people who have devoted their careers
to kids / edited by Marshall Duke and Sara Duke.
    p. cm.
Includes bibliographical references.
  ISBN 1-56145-200-9 (alk. paper)
1. Child welfare. 2. Children—Services for. 3. Child rearing.
4. Parent and child 5. Child care workers. I. Duke, Marshall P. II. Duke, Sara
HV713.W46 2000
362.7—dc21
                                                              00-009065

Table of Contents

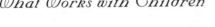

Part Two

WHAT TO DO?
SPECIFIC ISSUES IN CHILDREARING

75

Part Three

WHAT IS IMPORTANT TO US?
GUIDING AND SHAPING OUR CHILDREN

Introduction

There are many ways of knowing. One of our *beloved grandparents used to repeat this phrase again and again:* "We don't learn everything from books; life teaches us most lessons." Somehow that invocation of a second way of knowing—the experiential—has appealed to us more and more over the years. As a clinical psychologist and a learning disabilities specialist, both of us have spent our careers working with children, and we have known many other professionals who have devoted their lives to helping children. It is their wisdom—the lessons they have learned from life—that we sought out to record in this book.

The idea for the project arose from two sources. First, we observed that when we spoke with other professionals about individual cases involving particular children, we rarely got around to articulating what we thought really mattered. We also remembered how as young parents we were so wrapped up in the everyday details and struggles of raising our children that we seldom stepped back and considered the larger issues of parenthood. We knew much more when dealing with our grandchildren than we did when our children were growing up.

Both as parents and as professionals, we—and many others—had learned much along the way (humility and humor being high on the list!). We believed that this knowledge born of experience—this wisdom—could and should be harvested.

The second source of inspiration for the project was the Last Lecture Series offered by many colleges and universities across America. In the series, professors are asked to imagine that they are about to give the last lecture of their life. In this lecture, they are to address this question:

Based on all your years and experiences in your field of study, what would you want to pass on to the next generation?

Freed from the constraints of specific evidence, the lecturers are encouraged to take a more personal view of what their disciplines can teach us about our lives. Although the premise for the series is a simple one, it often yields astonishing and invigorating insights. We decided to pose this question to people who have spent their careers working with children. Scientific studies of child behavior and development abound; a host of experts are constantly ready to give us advice. But we were interested in another class of experts—people with a vast range of experience not only in working with children but also in simply living and conversing with them. We were convinced that such a collection of "last lectures" might both guide and enrich the efforts of adults to educate children and care for them more wisely.

Our hope was to gather the thoughts and reflections of people who were experts in some aspect of working with children and to put their insights together in a volume for parents as well as for others who work with children. We sought the help of a select group of professionals—people who had worked with children or adolescents for at least twenty-five years and who were known to be especially good at what they do. We asked these professionals—educators, pediatricians, psychologists, psychiatrists, ministers, librarians, and coaches, among others—to write a brief essay, a "last lecture," reflecting on what they had learned about kids. We ultimately obtained essays from forty people who had spent their distinguished careers working with and learning about children—their rich store of experience adds up to a thousand years of collected wisdom on raising children.

Here then is the wisdom from some wonderful people who gave of their time and energy to pass on to us what they have learned about working with children. While all of the contributions are meant for parents, professionals who work with children may also find them enlightening.

Different readers will seek and find different things in the thoughts of others. We leave it to you to decide which bits of wisdom you will make your own.

That's the beauty of wisdom—it's not a set of specific ideas. It is broad insight derived from extraordinarily thoughtful reflection on ordinary experience, combined with the ability to convey that insight in ways that touch the lives of others for the good.

We have great faith that the love of parents and the resilience of children enable most kids to grow up as effective and well-adjusted adults. But parenthood is a journey with many detours and dead ends. Just as on any other long trip, a couple of books along the way will at the very least help pass the time. Now and then, however, you may find a book that helps you discover sights that you might not otherwise have seen or that directs you to a scenic byway that you will remember forever. We hope this book can be one of those.

What Do Children Need?

PART ONE

Creating an Environment

for Healthy Growth

Children are like seedlings. They have *the potential to grow, flower, and bear fruit,* but unless they are nurtured in the proper soil and treated with care, they may not flourish. Many of our contributors addressed the question of the "soil" in which we raise our children. They remind us that a child's environment is a central concern. Too often, we as parents focus on what we are doing with our children and fail to attend to the atmosphere that surrounds them.

All parents want to provide a rich and nurturing environment for their children. Somewhere between the warm, inviting hearth of Norman Rockwell's America and the isolation of the rear seat of a VCR-equipped minivan, we must find that happy place.

Mankind owes to the child
the best it has to give.

—opening words of
THE UNITED NATIONS'
Declaration of the Rights of the Child

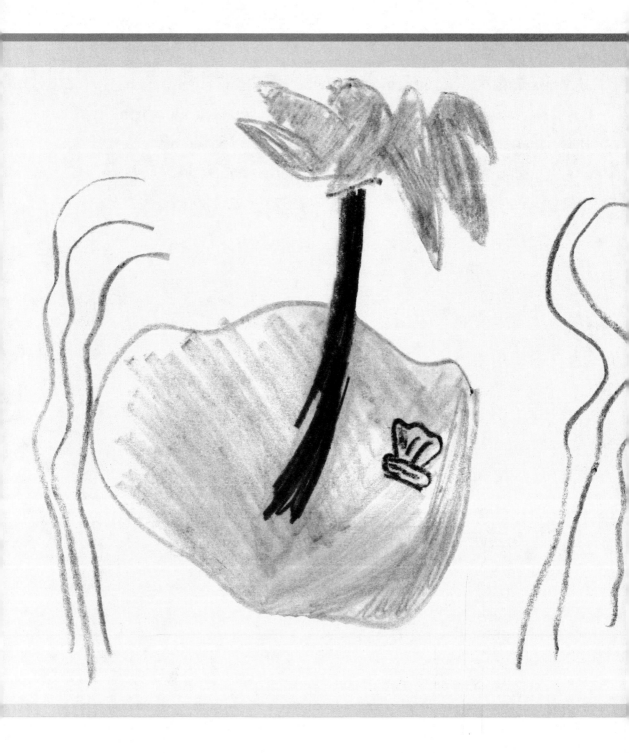

James M. Bennett

Ripples Upon the Water

Throw a stone into a pond. Watch the *ripples upon the water* spread out in concentric circles, ever widening, ever more subtle, ever more distant. So it is with raising children. Everything we do or say as parents, teachers, and friends has an immediate and profound impact upon our children. As children grow older, the effects of our interactions with them become ever more subtle, ever more distant. The impact of our words and actions remains, however, as does the awesome responsibility for starting the ripples in the first place.

Raising a child is a privilege. All of us as parent, teacher, coach, advisor, counselor, friend, and stranger ought to remember this every time we interact with children. Each child is a precious miracle, and each moment of encounter with a child is precious as well. Nothing we say or do is irrelevant. Every word and deed counts. I wish someone had taught me this before I became a parent. As many people before me, though, I had to find this wisdom for myself, learning from my mistakes as well as from my successes. Through teaching other people's children and through striving to be the best father I can possibly be, I have learned the following fundamental truths.

Every child counts. Every child comes into this world with a right to dignity and respect. In our interactions with our children, the children of others, and with each other, we must never lose sight of this truth. No child is more important than any other, and no child deserves less respect or dignity than any other. Every child is equally valuable.

Every moment counts. There are no irrelevant encounters with children. The way we say a groggy "good morning" to our children matters as much in the long run as the life lessons we teach in our most coherent and profound conversations. Children often care about moments we may consider to be trivial as much or more than they care about contrived formal encounters we see as significant. As parents or teachers we try to construct experiences that will lead, in our fondest dreams, to wonderful memories for our children. The truth is, however, that for most children, the daily interactions are much more important and memorable than the once-in-a-lifetime trips, events, or experiences we think matter so much. Children remember far more the conversations around the dinner table, the laughter and smiles of the impromptu moments together, than those "important" times that seemed so meaningful to us as they unfolded.

Children learn by example. The old saw, "Do as I say, not as I do," is tragically flawed. What we do is of utmost importance to our children. What we say matters as well, but what we do will shape the lives of those who stand by watching and learning.

There is nothing more important than love. Ultimately, things do not matter to children. Love does. Things are of this world and therefore fleeting. Love is spiritual and therefore permanent. We must not teach our children to love things and use people. We must teach them to love people and use things. And our love for our children must be unconditional.

Listen more than you talk. Instead of assuming that our children need to hear us talking more—telling them, lecturing them—we need to listen. Our children need to know that they can always come to us and find us there, ready to hear them, truly hear them. Children need to know that sometimes we will listen without interrupting and without judging.

Hugs and kisses mean more than words. Children are never too old to be hugged and kissed, even if they say they are. Sometimes our affection may embarrass our children for the moment, but the lasting message of the hug is far more important.

Encourage children to play, to laugh, to smile, to dance, to sing, to cry. And play, laugh, smile, dance, sing, and cry with them. At no time in our lives are we more uninhibited than when we are children. Let your children remind you how to express emotion, how to express joy, sorrow, and love.

Throw a stone into a pond. Watch the ripples upon the water spread out in concentric circles, ever widening, ever more subtle, ever more distant. Then think about the impact we have on our children. Children are precious. It is our task and our privilege to take seriously the awesome responsibility we share in raising them.

James M. Bennett *was born in Boston and received a B.A. from Indiana University and an M.A.H.L. from the Hebrew Union College, Jewish Institute of Religion. For years he has been a rabbi in Charlotte, North Carolina, and served as assistant director and teacher at Goldman Union Camp Institute. He is an avid sports fan, especially of baseball, and enjoys storytelling and folksinging. James and his wife, Amy, have three young children.*

Ora L. Hill Cooks

"I Need a Body"

It was a typical, late December weekend *night in the Southeast: cold, windy, and wet.* And we were a typical group of longtime friends renewing our camaraderie during a very competitive bid whist card game. The older children got to stay up, watch the card game and learn, and the younger ones went to bed at ten o'clock—no exceptions. It was usually the job of the host parents to put the youngsters to bed while the rest of us continued the card game. This particular gathering was at my home. As hostess, I completed my bed-down duties with the five youngsters, including my own six-year-old daughter, and happily returned to being a sideline instigator at the card game. After a few minutes, my daughter was standing in the hall door.

"Carla, what are you doing up?" I asked her. "I gave you everything already. What else do you need?"

Leaning sadly on the door frame, with her thumb halfway in her mouth, Carla replied, "It's cold. I need a body!"

Everyone broke into wild laughter and began making somewhat ribald comments on the wisdom and practicality of having a body close by to warm the cold, winter night.

Carla's God-Dad, Roy, put her on his lap, tucked her feet into the bottom of her long gown, put a blanket around her and said, "Carla, I know what you mean. There comes a time in life when everyone needs a body."

Carla went back to sleep wrapped in the warm body of her God-Dad's love, empathy, and protection for the rest of the evening.

The wisdom and practicality of needing and having "a body" to warm a young life is what I want to discuss here. When all the recent tragedies are analyzed, the situations reviewed, and the actions or lack of same detailed, I believe one fact will remain prime: children need "a body" to be there. Children need a parent's warm, enveloping body to ward off the coldness of insecurity, to shelter them from negative elements both natural and manmade, and to shed light on the dark images that can shadow their life experiences.

What can we do to provide "a body" for children when they need one? In my thirty-plus years as a teacher and parent who actively participated in the lives of the children I came in contact with, I have observed three factors that have tremendous influence in providing "a body" that helps children grow in a positive sense of self, productivity, and happiness: adult presence, encouragement, and joy. Although these are simple concepts, they are included in the writings of many renowned child study experts dating from John Amos Comenius (1632) to Albert Bandura (1977) and Darlene and Derek Hopson (1990), among others. Yes, these are simple concepts, and as John Dewey said, the simple is difficult to act upon. Having discovered the simple truth that a child needs "a body"—a hug or a cuddle—we can do the difficult task and act on that knowledge. We can provide "a body" of adult presence, encouragement, and joy to ward off the cold and darkness that can veil and envelop a young life.

Providing "a body" doesn't have to be physical. You can pay attention to what your children are doing, or not doing, and thus provide an adult presence in their lives. When you acknowledge children by saying "hi" and commenting on positive behaviors, you become a very powerful presence in their lives and provide "a body" that is affirming. Adult presence is as elementary as openly acknowledging the child's presence, complimenting him on a good behavior, giving her a smile or a wave. These simple gestures make impressions that can have a life-long influence on the development of a child's positive sense of self. These simple actions will be remembered for a long time and will provide "a body" of memories to soften the tough times experienced later in life.

Why do I make such a big deal of something as unpretentious as encouragement? As Dewey said, to act on the simple is a difficult task. Giving encouragement is a very elementary concept, but it must be done consciously on a daily basis to be effective. Each of us can recall the difference encouragement made at some point in our lives. But how many of us consciously take time to encourage a child? Praise, a pat on the back, or a simple "Keep

> " *To experience joy, a child must have basic needs met and be free of anxiety.* "

trying, you can do it" can make a tremendous difference in a child's success.

Of the three acts that I believe are essential to provide "a body" that children need, joy may be the most crucial one. But doing something that brings joy to a child's life is not easy. Childhood is a time and place when we need to experience the joy of simply rolling down a grassy slope, imagining exotic creatures in white cloudscapes against a clear blue sky, or laughing wildly after whirling around until the world turns upside-down and tilts. These are some of the small keys to the joys of childhood, and every child needs "a body" of these joys to take out and examine when life gets tough, as it inevitably will later. To experience joy, a child must have basic needs met and be free of anxiety. Childhood should be a carefree time and place.

Adult presence, encouragement, and joy are positive responses to the plea, "I need a body!" We can answer a simple request by taking some simple actions, but as we know, the simple is difficult to act upon.

Ora L. Hill Cooks *is Professor of Education at Clark Atlanta University. Born in Marion, Arkansas, Ora received her B.S. from the University of Arkansas in 1967 and her Ed.D. from Atlanta University in 1980. In her thirty-plus years working with children, Ora has taught in elementary school, high school, and college. When she is not writing, teaching, or speaking to groups, Ora enjoys flower gardening and playing bid whist. She has two grown children.*

Howard L. Weinberger

Lessons from
School and Life

As a long-term faculty member in a medical school, I have had the opportunity to interact with thousands of students over the course of my career. The students who stand out in my classes express or demonstrate certain characteristics, which they have learned from their parents or teachers, or both. We as parents and teachers do a great service to our children if we model for them and encourage them to express the following attitudes both in and out of school.

An enthusiasm for lifelong learning. The students who are most successful and are most enjoyable to teach are those who come to class already eager to learn. Once they graduate from school, those who continue to challenge themselves will broaden their horizons.

Curiosity. Along with an enthusiasm for learning, one of the most successful characteristics for success in school is curiosity—for the unusual and about the nuances of our daily encounters and the world around us. As a pediatrician, it is exciting for me to watch the development of young children as they begin to explore their universe from the toddler's first step to the teenager's developing sense of independence.

> **" Being able to look for the humor in situations helps adults and children alike to put things in perspective. "**

When given the opportunity, their curiosity is insatiable. Dull classes often can take the excitement out of a subject, but a student who remains inquisitive will flourish in those classes and as an adult.

A sense of humor. If we don't look for the humor in situations, then both we and our children will be miserable. For example, as a pediatrician I learned quickly that I could not take myself too seriously. Who else in medicine could get peed on, thrown up on, and pooped on and still enjoy working with children? Who else would spend four years in college, four years in medical school, and an additional three years for further specialty training—all to be able to talk seriously with parents about spitting up, sleep problems, and the best way to do potty training? Being able to look for the humor in situations helps adults and children alike to put things in perspective.

An open mind. Listen and don't jump to conclusions. It's very easy to assume that we as adults and as parents have all the answers and that we understand our children's concerns, but most of the time we don't. We need to take the time to listen to what our children are saying and to ask open-ended questions—that is, questions that require answers more than just yes or no—to encourage our children to express what is really on their minds. If we show our children respect by listening closely to them, then they will do the same to others.

These four ways to approach life and learning benefit us as parents as well as our children as they develop and progress through school and into adulthood.

Howard L. Weinberger, *born in Jersey City, New Jersey, received a B.S. degree from the University of Michigan and an M.D. from the State University of New York at Syracuse, where he is now Professor of Pediatrics at the Health Sciences Center. In his over thirty-five years on the faculty, he has served as director of Pediatric Ambulatory Services and now chair of Pediatrics. Howard is widely published in pediatrics. He and his wife, Anita (also a contributor to this volume), have three children. In his spare time Howard enjoys tennis and gardening.*

What we want is to see
the child in pursuit of
knowledge, and not
knowledge in pursuit
of the child.

—GEORGE BERNARD SHAW

Kathleen A. Walton

Raising Responsible, Cooperative, and Caring Children

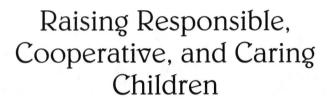

As a teacher, consultant, and childcare administrator, I have instructed *parents and teachers* about the child-rearing techniques developed by psychologist Alfred Adler. An Adlerian approach to raising children is effective at teaching children responsibility, cooperation, and concern for other people.

As a parent, I had the pleasure of using Adler's child-rearing methods successfully with my own four children, and now I see my children using the techniques with my seven grandchildren. I offer the following brief synopsis of Adler's thought, which contains a great deal of wisdom for parents today.

The best way to teach responsibility is to give it. Children, like adults, learn best by experience. But both coercive parents (those who wish to strictly control their children or make them do things) and pampering parents (those who overprotect their children) have great difficulty in letting their children experience the consequences of their behavior. Both the coercive and the pampering parent fail to teach children responsibility for their own behavior because, in both cases, the parents take responsibility for the child's behavior. The guideline to teach a child responsibility, therefore, is *Never do for children on a regular basis what they can do for themselves.*

> **"***Our current social environment tends to overprotect children....***"**

Encourage your children to try new things. Be enthusiastic. Let them learn from their mistakes. When they do make a mistake, ask questions such as "I wonder what else you might have done?" or "What would have happened if you had tried it this way instead?" Share mistakes that you have made. A good guide for parents to use in dealing with children is to ask, "How would I treat a friend in this situation?" For no reason whatsoever, invite your child to take a walk with you or play a game with you. The message you send to your children is that you respect them as fellow human beings and that you like them just the way they are.

Evaluate your child frequently because children's ability to do things for themselves changes quickly. Most parents underestimate what their children can do. Our current social environment tends to overprotect children and underestimate what they can do. Children are excited when they learn to do something for themselves. They feel encouraged when we ask them to do activities and chores that seem beyond their years. Don't rob children of this excitement and encouragement by doing for them what they can do for themselves.

Cooperation grows out of respect. Children are far more likely to learn to cooperate with us as parents (and eventually with each other) when we use respectful techniques that invite their cooperation. Two of the most common reasons why children refuse to cooperate with us are to gain special attention or to demonstrate their power. Pampering parents give their children unnecessary attention and so teach them to expect special attention or services. These children are ill prepared to cooperate with other children and adults. Coercive parents invite resistance from their children, and in the resulting power struggle, neither child nor parent wins. The guideline for teaching cooperative behavior, therefore, is to *attend to the behavior you want to teach.*

Parents who focus on cooperative behavior in their children teach their children to be cooperative. Parents who minimize their reaction to uncooperative behaviors reduce the likelihood that their children will continue to use such behaviors to gain recognition. Play with your child and have fun as a family. Being friends and having fun together sets an atmosphere that increases the likelihood your children will be cooperative when asked to do something. When a child has had a challenging day, parents need to "catch" the child being cooperative, or invite him or her to participate in a helping activity to refocus attention on cooperative behavior.

Parents who are respectful of their children and involve their children in decision-making processes suitable to the children's ages and abilities raise children who are willing to cooperate. These decisions might involve questions for young children such as "Would you like to wear your blue shorts or green shorts?" or for older children, "Which of the jobs on the job chart would you like to do?" or "Would you like to do your homework before or after dinner?"

To teach caring, show you care. Parents have a responsibility to teach children concern for other family members, for other members of society, and for the environment. We teach this quality by displaying it ourselves. Parents are children's first models for caring behavior. Ask yourself, "Am I kind to family members and others on a regular basis?" Place value on caring behaviors among siblings. Parents who recognize siblings who share and play together cooperatively promote the attribute of kindness.

Invite children to assist you with simple tasks. Thank them afterward and recognize their contribution. Let children know that helping behaviors are important. As a family, work together on a project that helps others. Collect items for needy people in your community or for people who have experienced a disaster. Talk with your children about news items that feature people helping others.

Be respectful of other cultures and nationalities in your conversations with your children. Share information about positive contributions of those nationalities and cultures.

Teach your children to be environmentally concerned. Involve them in recycling and other ecologically sound household activities. Read articles to them about the environment. Be a good teacher and example for your children.

Modeling these behaviors—that is, being responsible and cooperative and showing respect and concern—teaches your children to act this way as well and fosters a strong friendship with your children. Remember that being a parent means working yourself out of a job. *Free your children to be independent! Keep them as friends!*

Kathleen A. Walton *grew up in Fremont, Ohio, and received a B.A. in early childhood education from the University of South Carolina. She has taught first and second grades and has served as a consultant in early childhood education and parenting. Kathleen and her husband, Francis, who is a psychologist, have four grown children and seven grandchildren. In her leisure time she enjoys playing tennis, skiing, and traveling.*

Where parents do too much for
their children, the children will
not do much for themselves.

—ELBERT HUBBARD
The Notebook of Elbert Hubbard

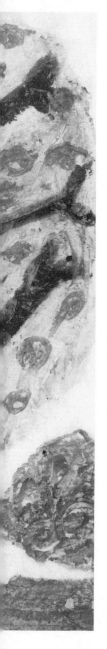

Lynn W. Brandon

Laying the Groundwork
for Success in School

A re children really different today from those who started school a generation or two ago? Certainly some things have changed the educational experience now from what it was in the past. Computers are a good example. But basic needs still are present in the life of any student, if that student is to become a successful, productive, and happy citizen with a strong identity. The cornerstones of a successful life identity are very simple and very basic, and students who experience them really do have a greater opportunity to enter adulthood armed with the necessary tools to survive. These cornerstones are a stable home life, a sense of community, and the possession of a faith.

Each individual needs the security of an identity. Today there is often a great rush to say that what each student needs is healthy self-esteem. But self-esteem is not something that can be taken off a shelf and handed to an individual. Self-esteem (liking who you are) is part of identity (knowing who you are), which must be developed one day at a time. Life experiences show us who and what we are, and help us understand how we feel about what we have contributed to life as we progress through it. Every child deserves to be treated with kindness and with a sense of expectation from parents and teachers. Caring, kindness, and expectations from adults convince the child that he or she is an individual of worth and can be successful.

Children are not responsible for the kind of home they live in, but they certainly either benefit or suffer greatly from that environment. Ideally the home should be filled with love—and love that is based on expectations. Children absolutely must come to school with the understanding that, no matter where they wish to travel in life, school is where they get their ticket. They need to understand from a very early age that school is their job and that, like other jobs, the better it is done the greater the rewards are.

A very wise person once wrote, "No man is an island." Children must learn to live in the world with other people, and it is in the family and the schoolroom where an enormous amount of that learning must take place. Living and learning with others teaches an individual how to behave appropriately. It develops an individual's conscience, which enables that girl or boy to become a part of a community that exists for the good of all. Children need to learn the job of giving to the community by becoming a guardian of its values and missions. They also need to know that the community exists to help them in time of need.

The development of faith in the life of a child is the role of the parents, not the school, and is, perhaps, the most significant thing that parents can do to ensure their child's success in both school and life. Through faith each person learns to acknowledge the existence of a Supreme Being, and that acknowledgment positions the individual in the proper relationship with other human beings. It also becomes the basis for the development of the student's understanding of what is the moral right or wrong for his or her behavior and the development of a personal character.

Regardless of what era they grow up in, children have the greatest advantage, not just in school but also in life, if they attend school (1) from a home where love is unconditional but based on the expectation that children must do their best; (2) in a community that expects its members to work, contribute, and behave for the common good; and (3) with a personal faith that is based on the security of knowing that a higher source knows and accepts them. These life cornerstones must all be provided by an adult in the life of a child.

Lynn W. Brandon *earned his B.S. degree from Tennessee Wesleyan College in 1961 and his Ph.D. from Georgia State University in 1981. He is currently Educator/ Counseling Coordinator for one of the three largest school systems in the state of Georgia. In his almost forty years of working with children, Lynn has been an elementary school teacher, a high school counselor, and a school system administrator. Lynn is a widely sought-after public speaker, but he also enjoys the quiet solitude of woodworking and gardening. He and his wife, Jane, are the parents of three grown daughters and have two grandchildren.*

Irwin Jay Knopf

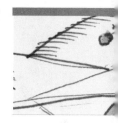

Enabling Your Child to Grow Strong, Happy, and Confident

The thought of preparing an essay offering advice to parents never occurred to me until I decided to retire. Even then, only a fool would agree to accept the complex and impossible task of dissecting and distilling either his own experience as a parent or his life's work in child development into a mere thousand words. Yet the prospect of helping parents rear healthy, emotionally stable, happy and effective, functioning children is so compelling that I could do nothing but accept the challenge.

In spite of the widespread acceptance of the idea that there is no single formula for successful parenting and child rearing, I truly believe, after almost fifty years as a teacher, researcher, clinician, husband, father, and grandfather, that I can package some of the major parental ingredients that can help parents and children grow to their full potential.

Approach the decision to become a parent with great seriousness. Successful child rearing begins with a couple who love, respect, and are committed to each other, and who have thoughtfully made the decision that they want a child. Their resolve to become parents should be the outgrowth of carefully considered discussions, disclosures, and agreements with respect to their values, needs, plans for the future, and the acceptance of roles and responsibilities vis-à-vis each other and the child. A decision to conceive a baby to force a marriage to take place, to repair a damaged marriage, or to satisfy the needs of one parent and not the other tends to negatively cloud and impair parent-child relationships. However, adverse effects are less likely to occur with unplanned conceptions if the couple have a stable, loving, and committed relationship and participate in the dialogue, discussion, and agreements noted above.

Protect your child's health. From the beginning of a pregnancy, a couple should seek out prenatal obstetrical care that monitors mother and fetus at regular intervals until birth. Medical care is necessary to minimize birth complications, to increase the probability of normal development of the baby, and to safeguard the mother's health. The new parents should then follow up with postnatal pediatric care to deal with sleep and feeding patterns, inoculations, and early diagnosis and treatment of illnesses. Talking to a pediatrician will increase parental understanding of their developing child and heighten their awareness of what the child can and cannot safely do and under what circumstances the child needs supervision.

Start early helping your child grow toward independence. Raising a child from infancy, of course, requires parents to be attentive and vigilant observers to keep the child out of harm's way and to meet his or her needs. However, parents must encourage their child to gradually become more independent, and they should guard against being overbearing and overprotective. As soon as parents see that certain activities or behaviors are in the child's response repertoire, they should allow the child to function on his or her own.

Praise your child for doing things on his or her own. Parents and other caretakers should warmly recognize and reward the child's success in acquiring a new skill or a desirable behavior in age-appropriate and tangible ways. These acquisitions, in turn, will facilitate the emergence of new independent behaviors, encourage further trials and successes, and promote the development of a wholesome and favorable sense of self-worth.

Establish age-appropriate expectations for your child at each stage of development. Parents need to know their child and to become familiar with the normal age range of emerging behaviors in order to establish realistic age-appropriate expectations. In instances where age-appropriate expectations are not used, parents are likely to communicate negative feelings of disappointment, failure, and criticism that tend to damage the child's self-esteem.

Express your love freely to your child. Most developing children can't get enough of parental love and acceptance that is evident in hugs, kisses, words of love and appreciation, and expressions of pride and delight. A home filled with love, emotional warmth, support, security, and a reward system consistently applied will not only increase the child's confidence in trying new and difficult tasks, but will also positively affect his or her self-worth. Children from a loving home are likely to develop a sensitivity to others; the capacity to love, to be loved, and to express their feelings openly; and the ability to establish meaningful interpersonal relationships.

Set limits for your child. As important as love is, it should not replace or interfere with the important parental tasks of setting and enforcing limits, consistently applying and following established rules, and even punishing the child when rules or limits are broken. Parents should not be intimidated by their child or fearful that he or she will not love them if limits are set and enforced. Neither a lack of guidelines nor excessive limits are best for the developing child. Choose a path someplace in or near the middle (moderation) for better and more effective results.

Talk with your child. Encourage your child to talk to you, but avoid the rut of asking questions that can be answered in a single word (usually yes or no). For example, instead of asking your child "Did you have a nice day?" or "Did you learn

anything new?" you will get more conversation if you ask "Tell me about what you did today" or "Share with me what you liked best today in school." Values are taught best by example and not by words. Encourage your children to talk to you and to see you as a person who will listen and whom they can trust with their concerns, happy news, or secrets.

Listen to your child. A parent needs to be a good listener—one who hears both the manifest and latent content of what is being said; one who is not judgmental, critical, or disapproving; and one who doesn't share the conversation with others unless the child gives prior permission.

Give your child necessary facts as he or she grows. Take the initiative and teach your child about sensitive subjects such as sex and intimacy instead of leaving it to friends, teachers, or others. Refrain from giving long and detailed answers to a child's questions unless he or she presses you to do so. Make sure your answers are age appropriate. Often, especially in matters of sex, a young child's interest is general and superficial. A complicated response may very well be much more than the child understands or wants to know.

Broaden and challenge your child's mind and imagination. Routinely expose your child to books, music, art, and science. Take him or her on field trips to museums, zoos, botanical gardens, historical events, and other places of interest in your community. Travel and learn together about different cultures and religions. Explore scientific findings and innovations together. Allow your child to learn about and participate in a range of recreational sports and activities.

Limit your child's time in front of a screen. In these days of electronic advances, parents often do battle with the pull of television and the attractiveness of computer games and browsing the web. Parents need to know what their child is watching on television and what he or she is doing on line. Monitor these activities carefully and set specific limits for them, leaving plenty of time for schoolwork, exercise, and free play.

Try not to fill all leisure time with structured and supervised activities. Avoid overloading the child with organized activities (no matter how beneficial they are) to the exclusion of free time for play with friends or the pursuit of his or her own interests. Some of today's children are so accustomed to having their after-school time planned and organized for them that they have difficulty playing on their own. When given free time, they tend to be bored, unhappy, and inclined to depend heavily on siblings or parents to entertain them. Make room in your child's daily schedule for some free time along with time for schoolwork, television, computer games, and participation in some structured and organized play.

> **"***Refrain from giving long and detailed answers to a child's questions unless he or she presses you to do so.***"**

Finally I say to all parents, thank God for blessing you with a child and perhaps in time with the wonderful gift of grandchildren. Take time to enjoy your child at every age and stage of development, because before you know it, he or she will be grown. Enriched by the wonders and joy of your child's every step and the incredible mountain of memories that are yours to relive and share, rejoice in the rewards of bringing that child into this world. In the end, you will be fulfilled and pleased with yourself because your parenting enabled your child to grow strong, to be happy, and to feel confident and comfortable with himself or herself.

Irwin Jay Knopf *received his B.A. from New York University and his M.A. and Ph.D. in psychology from Northwestern University. He has worked with troubled children and disturbed families for almost fifty years. Knopf served as head of the Department of Psychology at Emory University, was president of the Southeastern Psychological Association, and is Distinguished Professor Emeritus in Psychology at Emory University. He has written numerous articles and books dealing with children, including a textbook on childhood psychopathology that is a classic in the field. Jay and his wife, Roberta, have three children and many grandchildren. In his spare time he likes to travel, play a digital piano, and volunteer in the community.*

Jean Cline Pryor

Let Go with Love

Wisdom, to me, means drawing from experience, taking knowledge from others, living it, and using it to become the best I can be. My wisdom about children comes from being a parent, a teacher, and an observer.

As a mother I had the opportunity, many years ago, to prepare a brief speech on parenting. I chose to describe the magnitude of this job in a series of poems.

THE PARENT

Being a parent is…
Receiving and giving,
Correcting and praising,
Laughing and crying,
Showing and watching,
Always listening, always teaching—
Teaching our children how to love,
To have compassion, to set goals,
Then setting them free to be.

Remember what Abraham Lincoln said: "A child is. . . a person who is going to carry on what you have started. He is going to sit where you are sitting, and when you are gone, attend to those things which you think are important. He will assume control of your cities, states and nations. He is going to move in and take over your churches, schools, universities and corporations, All your books are going to be judged, praised or condemned by him, The fate of humanity is in his hands."

We prepare our children for their place in the world. We give strength, direction, and love; we build character through discipline and stability. We parents would do well, as Lincoln suggested, to think of our offspring as our successors. Their lives will flow on into the current of the future.

LETTING GO

A child is like a river.
　It runs in places prepared for it.
It moves over a bed of sand and rock,
　It splashes over shallows, flows deep;
When the rains come,
　It goes wherever the current takes it.
But if the banks hold strong,
　The river will one day leave its bed
　and flow bravely into the sea.

You as a parent, then, should prepare for both the gentle flowing of childhood and also the floods that come so unexpectedly. You can make a difference in who your child becomes, who your child will be, how well your child will adapt to life's ebbs and flows.

Decades of teaching have bestowed their own wisdom. In my years of preparation, I learned how to teach the *whole* child. To be able to instruct others, we have to know the subject or rules and enjoy the activities ourselves. We have to make what we are teaching important and fun. Over the years, styles have changed and what is taught in school has changed, but the children's needs have not changed. Teaching is still the same: to teach discipline, to accept discipline, and to be disciplined. It is important for all of us—parents, teachers, and other adults—to consider the whole child and how each child fits into our society.

GROWING STRONG

A child is like the plant called sea oats
That grows on the sandy beaches of the gulf.
This plant does not have the beauty of the rose.
Its colors are pale and hardly noticed.
But its slender blades bend before the ocean wind.
The waves surge over it and it doesn't break.

As they grow, the sea oats grasp the dunes.
Their roots bind the sand and other plants,
So joined, the mounds of grains stand strong.
The hill of sand with steadfast plants protects
All that is behind and around it.
The sea oats hold the sands together.

So it is with a child. In the beginning, the seedling is protected. When it matures, in turn it protects others. As parents and teachers, we nurture the child in hopes of raising a nurturing adult.

Let me offer one last bit of wisdom gleaned from lifelong observations of children and their families. A child comes to us ready to be what we can make it. If we are wise, we later let the child go with love to be what he or she can be. The choice is ours: to hold that being to us or let it go and watch it become what we prepared it to be.

To you parents, from a mother, a teacher, and an observer: Let them go with love, but never give up, never stop teaching, never stop loving.

SOARING

A new kite, paper thin, easily torn,
With strips of cloth tied together,
Hardly able to stand against the chair,
Leans unsteadily to one side.

But when a gust of air lifts it high,
It stretches its bold being heavenward.
It dips and glides, reaching high,
With colors flashing down to its glowing end.
Then it drops playfully before soaring up again.

There are two endings controlled by the cord
Binding this thing of flight to the earth.
One is to gather in the string.
The wind is lost, and the kite returns, as if defeated.
Another is to release it as it strains to reach higher
And to know it should be free.

Jean Cline Pryor *was born in Shelby County, Alabama. She received her B.S. degree in physical education and English from Alabama College in 1953 and her M.Ed. in physical science from the University of Montevallo in 1973. Jean taught physical education in school for thirty-two years, including serving as department head of physical education for the Shelby County Board of Education. She has also been actively engaged as a lay leader and speaker with the United Methodist Church. Jean was named Alabama Mother of the Year in 1983. After retiring, she has pursued writing, camping, singing, and being player/manager of a women's softball team. Jean has four children and seven grandchildren.*

Rita Myers Tuvlin

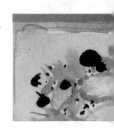

Creating an Ideal World

I'm working on creating an ideal world. In that ideal world people would not become parents until they are mature. By mature I mean knowing the rules of society and having the self-control to abide by them. Mature people respect one another and treat each other accordingly. They are not self-centered, and they have the ability to delay their own gratification.

In that hypothetical ideal world no one would have to raise a child without the help of at least one other mature individual—and, if possible, as many others as can be involved in a reasonably harmonious way. No one would use "It would be better for the children" as a reason for getting divorced. Parents, having brought children into the world unbidden, would accept the responsibility for learning how to get along with one another, foregoing personal happiness or fulfillment "for the sake of the children" if necessary.

Of course we do not live in an ideal world. All of us suffer from varying degrees of self-centeredness and lack of self-control. Few of us are fully mature when we become parents. But in spite of our imperfections, I believe that we can succeed at helping our children grow toward that ideal of maturity. And I believe that there are ways to make the difficult task of parenting a little less daunting. Calling upon my years of experience, I have come up with a few helpful suggestions to pass along to anyone who is—or is contemplating becoming—a parent. These words of wisdom, while perhaps not original, are so fundamental and so important that they bear repeating, over and over again.

It's okay to say no. You can nurture in your child the ability to delay gratification, an essential component of maturity, by the sensible and judicious use of the word no. Not no for the purpose of establishing control of a situation, nor no to get the child off your back, but a thoughtful no. "No, you can't have that because you don't need it and because we can't afford it" is an appropriate way to help your children learn to delay gratification. Children who grow up expecting their wishes to be fulfilled immediately will have much greater difficulty in becoming a mature adult.

Children need to know that certain behavior always results in certain consequences. When children fear the consequences of an action, they will learn to control their behavior. Instilling a fear of unpleasant consequences is an effective way to lead children away from inappropriate behavior—to make them do the things they need to but don't want to, or to make them refrain from doing things they ought not to do. Your goal as parent is, of course, to help your children reach the stage of maturity at which behavior is guided by internal guideposts, but until then, you must provide the external controls. Unfortunately, some people are slow to reach this level of maturity; some never attain it. Those individuals will always need the fear of consequences to keep their behavior in control.

Children need a sense of stability. Keep things constant and predictable in their world as much as is reasonably possible. This includes small daily routines and rituals, as well as the big issues, such as the people involved in their lives and the places where they live. Contrary to what you might think, this type of environment does not produce a rigid person. Children raised with stability are more likely than those whose formative years are erratic and unsure to become adults who are able to cope with change and insecurity.

Children need appropriate modeling of behavior. Children learn by imitation; they need constant exposure to the kinds of people and the kinds of actions you want them to imitate. Demonstrate to your children appropriate ways of interacting with and speaking to others. Avoid using sarcasm with young children, and establish clear rules about teasing. Never tease or allow teasing about sensitive subjects such as weight or eyeglasses. Teach your children that teasing is appropriate only when the people involved are feeling good about each other.

> **"Few of us are fully mature when we become parents."**

Having said that children learn by imitation, I must add that they also come to us "preprogrammed" with their own disposition and personality. If your child has difficulty in learning appropriate responses, talk about the problem with your pediatrician or another childcare professional.

Children need to get enough sleep (and so do parents). When parents seek advice from me about a child who is impulsive, inattentive, or unable to concentrate, one of the first questions I ask is "Does this child get enough sleep?" Attempt to establish and maintain a regular bedtime and wake-up time for yourself and for your children. All of us can function better with a sufficient amount of rest.

Know your children's abilities and adjust your expectations accordingly. When people get good results from hard work, their self-esteem grows. If you set children only at tasks that are too difficult for them, they will be discouraged. Conversely, if children only do easy tasks and achieve good results with very little effort, they will not progress and develop new skills. Ensuring good results from hard work is one of the most difficult jobs for a parent. You have to find that very narrow band of function—it is different for each child in each situation, and it is constantly changing—that is not too easy and not too hard. Parents must walk a narrow path between expecting too much and expecting too little of their children. Stay aware of your children's changing abilities and learn when and how hard to push.

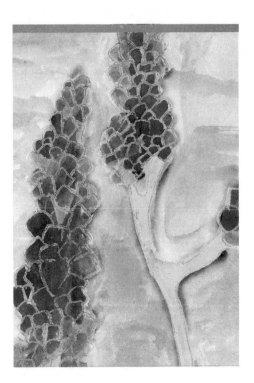

Be flexible. Sometimes a child needs a change of environment in order to be successful. This applies to academic and social situations. Often parents are reluctant to change their child's environment because they feel that "running away" from the problem will not solve it. While I agree with this concept, and certainly would not encourage continual changes in the hope of finding a better fit, I occasionally recommend a change that may have a very high probability of success. Our world is full of very different people and very different environments, and some of them fit together better than others.

Under no circumstances is it appropriate to allow a child to remain in an unsuccessful situation for a prolonged period of time. If a child is not experiencing success, it is imperative to work simultaneously on changing aspects of the child and the environment, both at home and school. This may include behavior modification, adjustments in academic expectations, parenting training, and the use of whatever professional resources are available. If these approaches do not result in any substantial improvement and a complete change of environment is not an option, then consideration should be given to a medical intervention if so indicated by the appropriate professional.

So, as you raise your children, I urge you to join me in pursuing that goal of creating an ideal world—a stable world of mature individuals whose behavior is governed by internal guideposts, a world of unselfish people who treat one another with respect. The goal may be unrealistic, but what's the point of becoming a parent if we don't at least try?

Rita Myers Tuvlin *was born in New York City, where she received her bachelor of science degree from City College of New York in 1964. She earned her master's in school counseling from Georgia State University in 1990. Rita has been an educator for almost thirty years, almost half of which she spent as a science teacher. She is currently a counselor at a private academy in Atlanta. Rita and her husband, Bernie (who plays trombone in a 1940s-style dance band), enjoy music, sports, reading, traveling, and being grandparents.*

Kay Gwaltney Remick

A Sense of Belonging

Who am I? How do I fit into this world? We must help our children find the answers to these two questions for themselves. Most of us have a deep desire to protect children from the world's tough realities, but we do them a great disservice if we do. A nurturing environment gives children the security to begin exploring who they are and how they fit into the scheme of things.

A newborn in a family is a gift received with thanks, love, awe, and a great sense of responsibility. When I became a grandmother for the first time not long ago, I couldn't help but think about the growing-up years of the new mother, my oldest daughter, and that of her sister and brother. In addition to being their parent, I have also been involved with children through my professional work as a children's librarian and, then, as a children's bookstore owner. As I take on my new role of grandmother, I find I do have some thoughts on the subject of what makes up that nurturing environment.

At the top of my list is a loving family—a family that shares meals, plays and reads together, takes trips together, and observes rituals. Before long that family has stories to remember and tell. It is in the telling and retelling of these stories that children learn and feel that they belong. If children have a sense of place—a sense of belonging—they will be ready to explore the wider world and gradually to become independent and self-reliant human beings. After all, isn't our goal as parents to give our children wings to fly? Here are some of the ways to meet that goal.

> **66** *Curiosity is an important ingredient in every child's development.* **99**

Listen to your children. Their questions need to be heard. Curiosity is an important ingredient in every child's development. It is sometimes hard to be a good listener, but a child receives a great deal of encouragement from this one simple act.

Spend time with your children. Time—not isolated "quality" units, but a lot of time—given to a child will produce great rewards. A garden doesn't grow just because you found time to plant the seeds. You must also spend hours watering the plants and weeding the ground to create space for growth. I often wonder why it comes as such a surprise to us that raising a child requires such an enormous amount of tender loving care.

Set limits and provide guidelines. I am convinced that children need and want limits, though they would never say this to the adults in their life. I have watched children get increasingly frustrated when they had no idea what they could and could not do. What were their boundaries? They didn't know. As children grow, they reach out further and further, but it is a gradual process. Don't give them more opportunities than they are ready to handle at their level of development.

Be consistent. It is certainly not easy to be consistent every time. Peer pressure is a powerful force that can challenge even the firmest parent's resolve. What parent hasn't heard this plea: "But Mom and Dad, everybody else is going!" And parents themselves can create a stumbling block when they fail to discuss events or issues between themselves ahead of time to determine how they feel about them. When parents speak with two voices instead of one, can you blame a kid for taking advantage of the moment?

Laugh with your children. Can you stop to smile when the going gets tough? I hope so, because it is often a sense of humor that gets a family through the turmoil and the difficult moments. When my own children were growing up, they didn't think I had been given my fair share of humor when it was being passed out. However, someone in the family group would always manage to see the lighter side. Before long everyone would be laughing, and we could discuss things in a less threatening way.

Talk with your children. In a healthy environment, there is not only laughter but also good conversation. Someone told me years ago that if you were still talking to your children when they were sixteen, then you were going to make it as a parent. I can't tell you how many times I have shared this little bit of wisdom with worried customers when they come into the bookstore. Parents need encouragement, too.

Russian composer Aleksandr Scriabin once said, "The universe resounds with the joyful cry I am." Every time a child is given the chance to grow up in a nurturing environment, then all of us can join in the celebration. A loving family creates stories to remember and tell, and in the telling of these stories a child knows that he or she belongs. Start laying this important foundation from the very beginning.

I look forward to grandmothering.

Kay Gwaltney Remick *received a bachelor's degree from Agnes Scott College, a master's in education from Virginia Commonwealth University, and a master's in library science from Catholic University. She has served as a children's librarian, on the board of governors for a private school, as a children's storyteller, and as docent for the school programs at the Virginia Museum of Fine Arts. She owns a bookstore in Richmond, specializing in children's literature, and has received national awards for the programs she holds at the store. She and her husband, Edward, have raised three children.*

48

Our children are not going to be just "our children"
—they are going to be other people's husbands and wives
and the parents of our grandchildren.

—MARY S. CALDERONE

Richard E. Hanson Jr.

"You Come Too"

Though I have spent my professional life as a practitioner rather than as an advice giver, I am pleased to have the opportunity to share a few observations with other parents—whether prospective, brand-new, or veteran— concerning literacy, achievement, tolerance, and teaching through sharing. I'd like you to consider four phrases.

"NOBODY TAUGHT ME TO READ."

By this statement I mean to express neither arrogance nor any lack of appreciation for my family or school environments. On the contrary, reading came to me naturally and easily, with no conscious exertion on my part, because I was surrounded by books, newspapers, and magazines, as well as by people who read or who read to me. It was clear to me early on that the marks on the page conveyed information or told a story. By the time I encountered an elementary school reader, I could see that it said, "Run, Spot, run." Before long, anything the library contained was availble to me.

The evidence is clear that when children grow up in an enriched and nurturing environment, many of them will learn to read on their own without much effort, some time between the ages of five and seven. If you are a parent, do as much as you can to provide such a setting at home. Let your child see you reading. Read to your nonreader. Encourage your new reader to read to you.

But literacy does not begin and end with our own children. If we as parents are serious about literacy for our children, it should follow that we would support early childhood learning environments for all children. Surely all of us benefit from richer learning opportunities for children in communities where families do not or cannot provide a stimulating home learning environment. I applaud efforts to intervene with poor or non-readers, but programs focused on third- and fourth-grade reading scores are treating symptoms, not causes. Let us aim to bring intervention even before first grade. I urge all parents not only to provide a learning environment for their own children, but also to advocate an early approach to preparation for literacy for all children.

> *Around the globe we witness the bloodshed caused by the clash of religious differences.*

"GOOD ENOUGH."

Thirty years ago I would have called this section "strive for excellence." That I choose not to do so is no repudiation of the general truth that it is our human nature to strive, to create, to build, to do—to the best of our abilities. We should demonstrate to our children that anything worth doing is worth doing well.

Nevertheless, youthful enthusiasm and a sense of infinite possibility eventually give way to an understanding that life is not just about striving for excellence. It is also about love and loss, about understanding amid confusion, and about acting in as responsible and caring a manner as possible. And sometimes, in spite of our fondest hopes and greatest investments, the question for us may not be one of excellence at all but rather one of survival itself, or even how we choose to face death.

In this framework we might wish for our children not only that they learn to strive, but also that they realize: that perfection is elusive, that understanding is always partial, and that sometimes what we think we want simply is not achievable. In some circumstances it is wise to accept that—given the resources available, given the time limitations, given our other responsibilities—just making the effort is "good enough." And our children may even occasionally discover that their best effort, though imperfect, nevertheless resulted in some outcome that was, surprisingly, much, much better than "good enough."

"I'M NOT SO SURE; WHAT DO YOU THINK?"

I'm still not sure just what my religious beliefs are. Although I am committed to acting responsibly toward myself and toward others, I am not always positive of the right word or action in every situation. It is hard for me to understand how people can be "certain" about their beliefs. In fact, I react viscerally when people insist their beliefs are right for me. I seem to make better progress in my search for understanding when I can discuss such matters with others in a spirit of questioning and inquiry.

Our country wisely separates government from religion. Our founders knew something about the evils of religious persecution, and generally there is a strong tradition in our country of religious toleration. Sometimes, however, we hear in the American political arena, or even closer to home, the voices of those who would impose their views on others. Around the globe we witness the bloodshed caused by the clash of religious differences.

As I read history, I see that many of the people who were "certain" were the assassins, the terrorists, the bigots, the fanatics, the inquisitors, and the executioners. The questioners have often been the poets, the pilgrims, the lovers, the martyrs, and the pardoners. What do we wish for our children?

Encourage in your children an open mind and a lively spirit of inquiry. Help them to pursue and examine the beliefs of their own traditions, while respecting the right of others to hold different views. Teach them to understand that life is more about questioning than about knowing the answer. Help them to see that sometimes we get farther along trying to figure out what God wants us to do than from petitioning God to be on our side.

Let us all read very carefully the labels on religious prescriptions of any kind—including the Ten Commandments or the Golden Rule. As I understand them, these labels say something like this: *For internal use only. Not to be given to others without proper authority.*

"THIS IS REALLY GOOD!"

Most of what I know and value and enjoy I have encountered through someone else. From my earliest days, parents and brother and sisters, and later, friends, family, teachers, classmates, colleagues—and sometimes, inadvertently, total strangers—continuously shared their enthusiasms, pointed out something interesting, said something, or acted in a way that led me down a new path.

And so it was that I first met the Heffalump, GREAT EXPECTATIONS, Psalm 139, honeysuckle, cell division seen under a microscope in a slice of onion root, a juicy peach, acorns, a bouquet of summer flowers in a hand-painted vase, the Beethoven symphonies, Dylan Thomas reading FERN HILL, a grandfatherly hug, the beatific mystery of a sixty-year relationship, pain patiently endured.

Each such gift of sharing brought me a relationship, an awareness of yet something else wonderful, and a joy that, I have discovered, is fun to share in turn.

As you go about the everyday routine of being a parent, I'd like to think you will keep these phrases in mind: "Nobody taught me to read," "Good enough," "I'm not so sure; what do you think?" and "This is really good!" While you're at it, maybe you'll come up with some handy phrases of your own.

But let us, above all, extend to our children—often enough that it matters—the poet Robert Frost's invitation in "The Pasture," *You come too.*

Richard E. Hanson Jr. *graduated from Harvard College in 1963 and earned his master's at Columbia University Teachers College in 1966. Now retired, he worked as a teacher and administrator in private schools for thirty-six years. He was the Founding Head of School at the New Atlanta Jewish Community High School. He and his wife, Cheryl, have two children. He enjoys reading, photography, and crossword puzzles.*

Dorothy M. Pearl

Allowing Children's Gifts to Emerge

$\mathcal{D}$*uring my career as an educator,* *I have had the opportunity to work with a wide* *spectrum of children.* Children of different ages offer an ever-changing set of challenges to parents and teachers. Whether you are raising children or teaching them, your methods and techniques must vary as the kids grow and move from basic skills to increasingly complex ones. Within each age group, some children have the ability to progress quickly; others need a lot of time and guidance. But regardless of a child's age and ability level, certain principles always apply. The thoughts I would like to share with you apply to all children—those who are gifted, those who are average, and those who are functioning at levels below their classmates.

Encourage. Watching your children grow is an exciting journey. Your children's interests and strengths emerge one by one, allowing you to get to know the unique individuals they are becoming. Whether your children demonstrate an interest in music, or mechanics, or sports, or language, encourage them, support them, and value them. Acknowledge and praise their strengths. We parents and teachers often have ideas about the kinds of interests we would like our children to pursue. Instead of limiting children's experiences to your own preferences, expose them to a variety of activities and cultural experiences at home and at school. Take care, though, to distinguish between *ex*posing and *im*posing.

Share. One of the most important things you can share with your child is reading. Begin reading to children at a very early age. Make books accessible to them. Let your children see you reading; that will convey the message that reading is important and enjoyable. Read your children anything that interests them as often as they want to hear it. Continue to read to them even after they have learned to read. Books can stimulate the imagination, lead to an appreciation of language, provide shared laughs, inform, and help a child deal with personal issues. If your child is troubled by something, go to the library and find a book that deals with a similar situation. Read the story together, discuss the characters in the book, and through that process you may be able to work through the child's concern.

Choose a television program to watch with your children. Talk about the program before, during, and after viewing. Stories they see on television with you may help them think about their own feelings, dilemmas, choices, and challenges.

Ask and listen. Help your children develop the ability to think analytically. Discovering things on their own is the best way for them to learn. When your children ask you a question, use the Biting-the-Tongue Technique. Don't respond immediately—allow some "wait time" and give them the opportunity to think and perhaps to discover the answer without any help from you.

When your children make a statement, use the same technique. Instead of breaking in immediately with your comments, ask them questions like "Why do you think that?" or "What makes you say that?" or "What could cause that to happen?"

> **"Never stifle thinking by responding to questions in a judgmental way."**

Encouraging children to think for themselves will lead them to try to solve problems on their own.

All children are naturally curious. They wonder about the world that they are discovering and ask many questions. Value their questions and treat them respectfully. Never stifle thinking by responding to questions in a judgmental way. We want our children to be curious, to wonder, to ask questions, to want to learn. It is all too easy to extinguish a child's enthusiasm with an impatient and negative response.

Value creativity. Some children demonstrate a natural penchant for creative thinking; others have to learn this skill. I believe that creative thinking can be taught. Many adults go through life convinced that they can't think creatively when actually they are just afraid of taking risks. Creative thinking requires offering ideas that have not been tested. It requires looking at something in a new and different way. Ask your children open-ended questions: "How are these fruits alike?" "How are they different?" Accept responses even though they may seem to make outrageous connections. Keep on hand a variety of throwaway materials—paper rolls, plastic bag ties, colored markers, paper—and ask your children to create something that has never been created before. Seek out good books that offer suggestions for encouraging creativity. Some children are naturally more creative than others, but every child can be creative on some level.

Build confidence. Having the confidence to take a risk now and then is a valuable asset at any stage in life. Creating a new product, offering a new theory, or merely suggesting a new approach to something involves taking risks such as looking or sounding different or going against the majority. Help your children gain the confidence to disagree with their peers on important issues. Help them attain the confidence to overcome the fear of making mistakes. The fear of making a mistake can paralyze a person when a decision is to be made. Help your children learn that everyone—even a parent—makes mistakes, and that all of us can learn from our mistakes.

Support education. Develop a partnership with your child's school and teachers. Educating children is a task of mutual concern. Discuss your child's needs with the appropriate personnel. Offer teachers as much information as they need to enable them to provide the best educational programming for your children. When possible, volunteer to assist a teacher. Each of you will develop a better understanding of the other's challenges.

After a lifetime of working with parents, teachers, and students, I feel privileged to share these ideas with a new generation, including my own children who now have families of their own.

Dorothy M. Pearl *earned her B.A. from Brooklyn College in 1955 and continued her graduate studies at Syracuse University. For more than twenty years she taught elementary school students who are gifted and talented. When she left the classroom, she continued working as a curriculum consultant for gifted programs. Until her retirement, Dorothy served as staff development facilitator for the Syracuse City Schools in New York. Both her husband and one of her two daughters are psychologists.*

Every child is an artist.
The problem is how to
remain an artist once
he grows up.

—PABLO PICASSO

Edward Z. Rosenzweig

A Work in Progress

At the beginning of my professional career in child psychology over a quarter century *ago,* I was certain of many truths. Fresh from graduate school and steeped in the scientific tradition, I quoted studies and theories and spoke with authority about expected behavior and developmental milestones. And above all, I remained the unbiased expert: I had had no children of my own and had not lived with a real, live child. I dispensed advice and wise counsel to all who would listen, and I prided myself on my authority.

Then, it happened—"it" being the birth of my own child and the dawning of a new understanding and wisdom. Fortunately, my son

had not read the same books and journals that I had, and so he did not do what he was supposed to do nor at what

> **"*...remember your own childhood.*"**

preordained moment he was to do it.

Oops! I was no longer the unbiased expert and authority. I now had to learn by and from experience and to figure out what worked for me and for us. This, then, is the first truth that I have discovered: Reading books as preparation for working, living, and dealing with children gives a comforting yet false security. Certainly, all the words and thoughts of the wise ones who came before are useful, but they should not be relied upon as the ultimate authority. Parents need to follow their own thoughts and instincts to love and enjoy their children.

The second truth I have learned is that children need empathy and understanding paired with limits and boundaries. To develop empathy, remember your own childhood—the joys, the pains, the innocence, and the wonder of encountering things for the first time. Recall the pleasure of firsts, but also the cost of them: that everything new brings a certain loss of innocence and is part of a child's inexorable march toward growth and maturity. It is the cost of finding out about the Tooth Fairy and Santa Claus and the fallibility of parents.

We cannot, and perhaps should not even want to, protect children from the myriad and contradictory experiences of childhood. But we must not willfully expose them to events that squelch the natural process or freeze them in their tracks. It is important to set limits and boundaries, to provide a safe but not constricting environment for children's experiences.

What is the third truth I have discovered? A sense of humor is crucial. It is the ability to see the many-sided nature of events and to greet those events (at least in time) with a certain amount of equanimity.

Parenting is a grand improvisation. We borrow the wisdom of others but only own it through experience. Stay involved and engaged in the process because it is a work in progress.

Edward Z. Rosenzweig *is a native of Savannah, Georgia. He received his bachelor's degree from the University of Virginia and his master's and doctorate in clinical psychology from Emory University. In his private practice in clinical psychology he has worked with children for more than twenty-five years and has taught undergraduate and graduate courses in psychology. Ed has served as a consultant to many hospitals and schools for children with special needs and has given presentations and published numerous articles on psychotherapy for children. In recent years he has expanded his work to include psychotherapy for men. In his spare time, Ed enjoys cooking, watercolor painting, and playing guitar. He and his wife, Barbara, have a son.*

Anita Weinberger

Positive Parenting

After twenty years as the director of a *program for three- and four-year-olds,* I have come to believe that the preschool years are the most important in your child's life. I offer the following suggestions as you do the most important job I know of—parenting.

Listen to your child. Good listening is crucial to communication. Children need to know that their parents are listening. When your children are talking to you, get down to their level and make eye contact with them. Involve yourself in conversations with your children. This can extend their thinking, vocabulary, and problem-solving skills. From time to time repeat what your youngster has just said to you. Responding to their words conveys mutual respect and encourages children to express their thoughts and feelings freely and honestly. Remember that we communicate with each other nonverbally as well as verbally. Our actions, facial expressions, and tone of voice let our kids know when we are listening to them. A smile, a nod, a frown, or a pat on the back can say a lot.

Be positive with your children. Put on a happy face as often as possible. When I interview candidates for teaching positions, the first thing I notice is a friendly smile. Children notice smiles, too. They need the reassurance of a warm, sympathetic face. Let your children hear affirming words. At least three times a day, use positive statements about their behavior, such as "I like the way you are helping to pick up the toys," "You're doing so well dressing yourself," or "I like the yellow, red, and green circles in your picture." Praise your children for specific accomplishments. Build your children's confidence by giving them credit for what they do.

Involve your children in creative activities. Keep on hand basic art supplies such as pencils, paper, crayons, paste, paints, scissors, Play-doh, and fabric scraps. Give your children the freedom to create. Always place the focus on the creative process rather than the end result. But when your children complete their projects, display their creations in a special area of your home at their eye level.

Take your children on short trips to parks, museums, the zoo, or the grocery store. Encourage them to explore using their five senses. On-site activities will increase your children's general knowledge and will give them a better understanding of the world. Be sure that the trips are age appropriate and match your youngster's attention span.

Be a secretary and record your children's thoughts after a trip or special event. Let your children be the author. After you take down the story, read it back to them, pointing out the words as you go. Eventually your child will read them to you. Even a very young child can design the book cover and create pictures to accompany the story.

Encourage imaginative play. Young children have vivid and active imaginations and enjoy devising imaginary friends and places. Pretend play not only stimulates children's imaginations, it also helps them make sense of and feel in control of their world.

Read! Read! Read! You can never read too much. Expose your children to a wide variety of books by many different authors. When reading to young children, be careful to choose books that are enjoyable, predictable, and meaningful to them. Encourage your children to "read the pictures" by putting their own words to the story. After a while they will memorize favorite books and eventually begin to read them on their own. When a child suddenly figures out the relationship between the sounds and the symbols, it is exciting indeed. Visit the library with your children often and let them help you select the books. Stories can nurture feelings of compassion and understanding between adults and children. A book may trigger questions such as "How did the character in the story feel about what happened to him?" or "What would you have done in this story?"

Sing! Sing! Sing! Bring joy to your children by singing with them. Most young children love to sing and to be sung to. Share songs and chants with your children daily, and encourage their natural musical aptitude. Expose them to singing, dancing, creative movement, playing rhythm instruments, and listening to music when they are very young. Search out some of the excellent music books and recordings created especially for young listeners. Look for songs that make use of repeated words, musical phrases, or rhythmic patterns. Kids love music and can learn songs and motions easily. As they master the vocabulary and melody of a song, they are gaining important learning skills.

Provide occasions for your children to hear classical music. To some extent, our children's tastes can be shaped by the music we play for them. In order for children to appreciate music of quality, they need to hear it played repeatedly. Try playing classical music recordings at naptime to create a restful atmosphere.

Be an advocate for your child in school. Get involved in your child's preschool and elementary school. Stay informed about what is happening in the classroom by offering to help the teacher and the students. If you are pleased with the school program, tell the teacher. If you have information that will help the teacher plan the best program for your child, share your thoughts. Administrators and teachers do not receive enough feedback from parents.

Create a loving home environment. Show your children every day that they are loved. Hold, hug, and kiss your youngsters. Ask for their help and opinions, and express appreciation for their efforts. Share responsibilities with them and catch them cooperating. When children are learning and contributing, they develop the positive self-image that will enable them to tackle life's problems. Cherish your time together and model those qualities that you want your children to possess. Promote kindness, truthfulness, honesty, and caring.

Being a parent is the most challenging and the most satisfying of all jobs. Children have boundless energy, inquisitive minds, and a desire to learn. They're honest, open, creative, enthusiastic, warm, and loving. Enjoy every moment with them, for as we all know, childhood passes too quickly.

Anita Weinberger, *born in New York, received her bachelor's degree from Syracuse University in 1956 and her master's in education from the University of Maryland in 1964. Anita, now retired, spent thirty years in education, serving as an elementary school teacher and principal. She also writes children's songs and has published over forty-two of them in such popular magazines as* Humpty Dumpty, Ranger Rick, *and* Grade Teacher. *In recognition of her special talents and qualities, Anita was named in 1973 as one of the Outstanding Elementary Teachers of America. She and her husband, Howard (also a contributor to this volume), have three children.*

Sara Bookman Duke

Before You Turn Around

In my work as a learning disabilities specialist, I have centered on educational issues. People usually come to me when things go wrong at school. Over the years as parents and I tried to work through their difficulties and as I stumbled through raising my own children, I hope I've garnered a few insights. I wish someone had shared these bits of wisdom with me when I had first had kids, and I'd like to pass them on now.

Don't let parenting just "happen" to you. I know when you are trying to talk on the phone and your kids are having a screaming battle, you think they will never grow up—but they do. You turn around and they are gone, and you realize that a thousand things you meant to tell them or do with them were never done. Time slips by in a whirlwind of activity and you are not even sure how that time was spent. I wish someone had reminded me how finite the time is when parents are intimately and constantly involved with their children.

Because there is only so much time, choices must be made. Take some of this precious time to sit down and think about what you are going to do with it. As parents we all make different choices. The question of what you choose to do with your family time is important, but it is even more important that you are conscious of your choices. Think about what you dream of for your children and make your time reflect that. There is only one Saturday afternoon a week—do you want to spend it at a soccer field, a piano lesson, or a museum? How about shopping, attending a movie together, or helping out in a soup kitchen? There is no "right" answer—nobody can be or do everything. But do not just let things happen. Think about what you value and what you want to transmit to your children and put your time there.

Choose to spend as much of *your* time as you can with your children. Even though you may not always be able to plan and schedule "meaningful" times with them, you can take advantage of the times you are together. Children will talk in the most unexpected moments; try not to miss those chances to listen and respond to them. There is simply no substitute for being with your children—a lot! (Yes, I was a working mother. No, I do not think a mother should quit work. Yes, I felt guilty.) I know this is hard. But keep in mind that the ways we choose to spend our time reflect our values. When we make time for something or someone, we show that this thing or this person is important to us. Be assured, your children realize this.

Know your child. Each child has different strengths and weaknesses and different tolerances. Some children want to be busy all the time; some might need an enormous amount of time alone. Some are good at sports and some at schoolwork. Most are average at many things. Experts in psychology speak of a child's inborn temperament. The reality is that all children are different, and some are just easier to raise than others. You are not going to be able to control what your children feel like and how they respond to situations, but you can try to know your child. Know what they can tolerate, know them as personalities, and know how they think. I've worked with thousands of kids—most of them have had some school difficulty—and I am convinced that, no matter what their IQ or their SAT might be, kids can make it just fine if they find a passion and learn to work and involve themselves in it. Your job is to help your children find their passions—those things that help them find out who they are, those things they can turn to when other things go wrong. All children need something that can lead them to be enthusiastic and interesting people and can give them, not just success, but goals and direction.

> **66** *Remember that school does not equal life.* **99**

Don't get hung up on learning issues. Little kids are just little kids. Knowing that your child is able to read by kindergarten may be nice and may be great for bragging, but early reading does not guarantee that your child is "smart." In fact, forcing a child to learn these skills too early may hinder other types of significant learning that contribute to a longer-lasting development. Helping the young child develop means talking to him and helping her to develop language and thinking skills. The young child does not need to learn numbers and letters. She needs to learn to think and enjoy life, to play and relate to other people. Every minute of parenting presents an opportunity for helping your child grow.

Remember that school does not equal life. Look back at my second point—know your child. Do not ever allow your child's performance in school to become the only issue and measure of the child. Not all kids can do well, and they all certainly can't perform at an A level. Children vary according to their Emotional Intelligence (as described by Daniel Goleman). Situations change, and your child's performance will vary according to the demands of a given school, grade, and teacher. There are very few Michael Jordans and very few Einsteins; most people manage to do just fine without being either. But being realistic about your child does not mean you do not expect effort and involvement. If school performance is of real concern to you, if you really care, do not just ask about grades; take an interest in what your children are learning, and show them that you respect the world of the mind.

If you sense something is wrong at school and are concerned, *trust your instincts.* Try to get help. Certainly most children will outgrow most problems, and there are some problems that cannot be solved, even with lots of help. But I have learned that parents are much more comfortable if they feel they have done all that they can do. Often a small tweaking of the system at home and school makes a big difference. By the way, doing all you can does not mean that you should insist that your child stay at the "best" school when he or she can remain there only with ongoing tutoring and endless stress. There are many ways to be happy and many ways to be success-ful. Do not force your child into a bad match. Help your child to find what is right for him or her.

Give your child a family. Each child needs more than parents—he needs a family, she needs a history, he needs to be linked. Children need to know that their family is the world's most special family. Help children see the unique importance of their own family, not to make them feel superior to others, but to give them some con-nection to other people, places, and times. It is a sense that the family counts—and that children are part of a unit and not isolated and alone in the world attending only to their own desires—that holds kids through the difficult times of being teenagers and enriches their lives as adults.

Give your child memories. Now that I am a grandparent, I have "quality" time to be with my grandchildren. I try to bear in mind what I once read—that this is time to pass on a legacy. When I tell my grandchildren things that happened to me when I was a child or stories my grandmother told me, I see their faces light up as they see how the stories connect to them. I wish everyone lived in a world surrounded by close relations who might help them in raising kids, but I know that this is unre-alistic. I also know that it is hard for busy parents, but still, please take the time to give your children memories. We *are* our memories. Our perception of our present world is related to what we remember, and of course what we remember is also related to our present perceptions. Everyone loves stories, especially ones that can relate to them. Give your children a history. Give them stories that are tender, that are funny, that are trite, that are melancholy—it doesn't really matter what kind. These stories will root them and bind them to other people.

As the makers of memories, parents' most useful tool is ritual. We cannot be sure what our children will remember, but as all educators know, repetition increases the chances that the memory will remain. Religious observances offer a rich heritage of meaningful rituals, but you can also make your own. The important thing is that you and your children begin to look forward to those rituals, to count on them. Eventually you will find that all of your lives are fuller for them, and that your children will want to pass them on to their own families one day.

Give your kids a community. It *does* take a village. It may be obvious by this point that I think the individual is much more comfortable when his or her importance is reinforced by being part of both a unique and a continuing chain. But I also believe that children need to feel responsible for and to something much bigger then themselves. Help your children be a part of a community, whether it is a church, a neighborhood, or a city. You can do this many ways, but do it so your children can be with people of different ages and economic levels. Give your children opportunities to do something for others—things that are meaningful and real. Teach them by example, but also *make* them learn to give of themselves.

Keep laughing. Parenting requires a lot of serious thought and hard work, but it is also a tremendous amount of fun. I have observed many families that work well together; the essential constant in all those families is the ability to laugh. Laughing together unites and heals. It definitely can save the relationship between parents and teenagers. Sharing moments of fun can allow both parents and kids to know that crises pass, and can help put things back in perspective. Bring your children up in a house that is filled with laughter and where humor reigns. Viewing life with joy enhances and enriches all positive experiences and provides strength to cope with the inevitable negative ones. I just read an article in the morning paper about how negative emotions are transmitted through the family, about how depression spreads from one person to another. According to the article, it is much easier to spread negative feelings than positive ones. Laughter and humor let your child

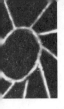

know the world can be a light and airy place. They make children feel safe and help build the coping skills to survive difficult times.

Each child is different and all children respond differently to their parents. But if you can, with humor and delight, transmit to your children a commitment to family, a belief that they share a special history, and the feeling that they are part of a larger community to which they bear a responsibility, you have given your children the underpinnings to become comfortable adults. Over the years I have seen highly structured and very loose families, very conservative and very liberal families, and I have realized that children can be raised well in many different ways. The details are not nearly as important as the commitment to each other and to the joy that life can offer.

Sara Bookman Duke, *a native of New Jersey who has lived in Atlanta for over thirty years, received a B.A. in history from Indiana University in 1964 and an M.M.Sc. in communicative disorders and learning disabilities from Emory University School of Medicine in 1979. Early in her career she worked at the Howard School for children with special needs and in 1987 began private practice as an educational consultant primarily involved in diagnostics, individualized program development, and identification of optimal school placements. She has worked with more than 2500 children and is a popular speaker before parent groups. Sara Duke and her husband, Marshall, have three children and five grandchildren. Her free time is spent reading, gardening, and worrying.*

What to Do?

Specific Issues

in Childrearing

The behaviorist John B. Watson once said that if he could have complete control of a child until the age of seven, he could produce any kind of adult that he wished. With what we now know about the importance of inborn temperament and the degree to which children play active roles in their own parenting, we are wise enough to realize that Watson's belief was not only ill-conceived, but impossible.

In the first place, no parent can interact in exactly the same way with different children. Every parent responds and reacts to different children in different ways. No two siblings, even twins, have the same parents.

Second, as our contributors attest, the guiding and shaping of a child is a two-way effort—a joint venture between parent and child. We have hopes for what our children can and will become, but all children cannot become everything we wish for them. Moreover, some of our children simply refuse to cooperate with our hopes for them.

When adults emerge from the cocoon we call childhood, outcomes are not easy to predict or to control, but the wisdom gleaned from centuries of experience seems to corroborate the following observations:

1) we have far less control than Watson assumed we had;

2) we have much more time to affect our children than the five years that Freud gave us;

3) most children are resilient enough to absorb our errors as parents; and

4) the nature/nurture controversy (is it the genes or is it the environment that controls what happens to our kids?) has no clear answer. Many contributors addressed the issue of guiding and shaping our children. And it shouldn't surprise you that they didn't all agree with one another!

Perry McArthur Butterfield

Love and Limits

My greatest joy and challenge in life has *been raising my children,* who are now fine adults with their own broods. My professional life has been spent as a researcher of the emotional development in infants and toddlers. This article is about setting limits. Although the examples used here are primarily about babies, setting limits applies to the baby, the older child, and to you and your own relationships with your peers.

I like to call limits guidelines. Guides help us find the way. When you set limits and expectations for your children, you are helping them find the way. Defining and maintaining limits is an act of love.

When you as a parent set limits for your children, you are preparing them to become self-controlled and self-reliant. This skill will benefit them throughout their lives. Limits at home prepare your children for limits in life. Young children become emotionally prepared for the challenges of peers and of school when their first limits have been lovingly set by parents. By establishing rules and guidelines for your children, you are teaching them values such as tolerance, respect, understanding, cleanliness, joyfulness, and courtesy.

The best time to begin setting limits is with your infant. At about three months of age, babies begin to notice that their cry is powerful enough to bring a parent to their side. Infants begin to know that their parents are there for them, and a special attachment begins to grow. When babies are fed, loved, diapered, and feeling drowsy, it is a time for sleep. Parents who begin quiet discipline by putting the baby into bed and leaving the room are making the first important step to communicating their guidelines or limits. These babies hear their nighttime music box, they see their teddy bear who lives in their crib, and they feel their special blanket. All of these things signal sleep.

Many babies at three months will cry a few times to see if a parent comes back, and then they settle down to quiet themselves for sleep. These babies learn that when parents say "no more," they mean it. An expectation has been set. The guidelines are clear: bed means sleep or quiet play alone.

These self-quieters are the babies who, as they grow older, are often very happy to be alone in bed. At night and in the morning they chirp and coo to their toys, practice words with their teddy bear, and later read books or practice walking around the crib till a parent comes to say "Good morning!" They have learned to go to sleep on their own, but also they have learned to enjoy being alone, and creating their own fun. They will use this ability throughout their lives.

The reverse of this situation is the baby whose parents feel that the child needs to be rocked to sleep every night. These babies become dependent on help to go to sleep. They will continue to need help moving from tired to asleep, perhaps even into adulthood. This pattern is appropriate for a preterm or small baby who is less neurologically developed at birth and has genuine trouble modulating from an alert or fussy state into a sleep state. Babies such as these may need many months of close body contact to be able to learn to self-quiet, but there will come a time when the limits will need to be set.

Do not let a genuine need for early support infect your total relationship with your child. All children need quiet discipline to learn to cope as adults. Your job as parent is not to do everything for your child; rather, it is to guide your child toward self-reliance.

The parent who has understood the value of clear, quiet discipline around sleep is usually the parent who uses this same skill for saying no to standing in the high chair or throwing food. By setting guidelines ("No, you must sit down") and helping the baby to sit, the baby has a pattern or model to follow. If the baby insists on standing, there is no argument: the parent simply puts the baby on the floor and the meal is over. There is no blaming, or anger, just clear, quiet action. If baby cries, ignore him.

Discipline is not about anger or shared negative emotions. Parents who are cross with their babies destroy their ability to teach. When faced with parental anger, the child experiences fear. Learning stops as the baby's brain reacts with strategies for escape and withdrawal. Setting limits must be done calmly, clearly, and consistently with little or no emotion or argument. Change your mood from fun to neutral, but not to anger.

> **" When faced with parental anger, the child experiences fear. Learning stops as the baby's brain reacts with strategies for escape and withdrawal. "**

If you as parent did not start early to set limits and establish discipline, you can always begin now. Alert your child that things will be changing. Discuss with the child that you need some help in making these changes. Discuss your needs, such as more personal time, more help with the household, more fun in your relationship with your child. Tell your child that you believe the whole family needs some structure and limits and that there are going to be more consistent rules for everyone. Explain further that by consistent you mean always the same: the rule will always stand, and you will not negotiate anymore. When you can begin setting reasonable limits, the expectations of your child will change. Your child will fuss about the new rules at first, but will quickly learn that you no longer give in when pushed. You may find it hard to endure some crying, whining, anger, and frustration from a child who is suddenly thwarted. Consistent limits means that you stay cool, calm, but committed.

There are a few secrets to making limits work. The first one is to keep your rules and guidelines few and simple. Be sure that these are manageable for your child. Are they understood? Are they logical and reasonable? Are they for safety or for the good of the group? Are you expecting too much for the child's developmental level?

Limits should be easy for the child. A child who is overwhelmed by rules will withdraw or become obstinate. Regardless of the child's age, begin each new task with clear, calm, consistent guidelines. The first time your child experiences something new, share that new experience with him. Set the rules or limits ahead of time.

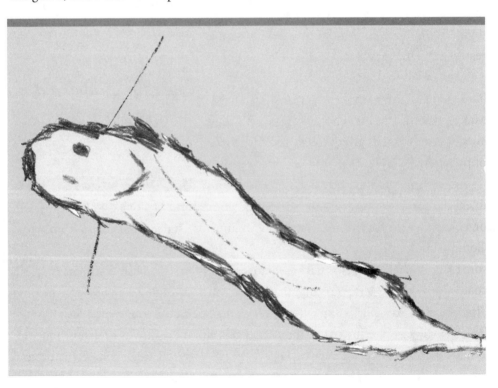

"We are going to Aunt Zelda's wedding and you will have to sit quietly for a long time while we watch her. When we are in the church, we need to be quiet. I will take some of your books to help you." Setting guidelines or rules is setting expectations. This helps the child.

When a limit has become part of the pattern of life, it will seem natural for the child. If you ask your child, "Please change into play clothes after school," expect that, at first, this may seem to be a chore for your child. But that chore will become a habit. The child internalizes the chore and it becomes a mastery skill. It feels good.

Another secret parenting tip is your participation with the toddler and young child. Do the hard stuff as well as the fun stuff together. This shared event or sense of "we" is a very useful parenting tool. With your toddler, it is obvious that you are literally as well as figuratively we. She is in your arms at the grocery, in your lap at church, in your plate at dinner. But she will also respond to limits if you seem to be sharing them. "We need to get ready for bed now." "We need to pick up these toys." "We need to stop running." "We need quiet time now. I'll read my book; you read your book."

A sense of participation is also important for the older child. Homework is very hard for a child when Dad says, "Go do your algebra; I'm going to watch the game." Managing your child's behavior is often a matter of managing your own behavior. Your child will copy what you do more than respond to your words or your threats of punishment.

A third secret of parenting is giving your child some power. Your children need to enjoy feeling a sense of autonomy. They grow and learn when they feel in control or competent. They need to accomplish goals and to feel ownership and pride. Consider this scenario: thirteen-month-old Isabelle is sitting on the stairs eating some Cheerios from her plastic bowl. Mom says, "Okay, it's time to go. Here is your coat." Isabelle pulls the bowl close to her and shakes her head no. Mom says, "Isabelle, we have to go!" Isabelle grips the bowl closer and screams as she shakes her head more firmly.

Autonomy is a deep inner need for all of us. We need to have our own goals, and we are driven to accomplish them and to fight for them. Children are no different.

Listen to your children. Let them be a part of the guidelines you set. For Isabelle, her need for power was focused on keeping and continuing to eat her Cheerios.

As parents, you will need to balance your children's drive to gain their goal with your need for limits. When Isabelle hugs her Cheerios to her chest, listen to her. Join her goal and then she will join yours. Think "we" and help her pack up the Cheerios in a plastic bag for her pocket. She will be very happy and satisfied to leave with you now. This possible argument was turned into a fun adventure and a learning task. Parent and child cooperated and adapted. Both persons' goals were accomplished.

Listening is at the heart of good parenting. Because we know that autonomy is important, it makes sense to ask your child how he or she feels about a situation. What would make following the rule easier? Is there a compromise? Isabelle's mom listened to her and compromised.

This is true throughout child rearing. Your child will always be at some developmental state that seems all-consuming. Whether it is dolls, soccer, CDs, or nail polish, it will be easier to limit and bring these into balance if you also allow for the child's needs to be expressed. Very few kids are maliciously bad; they are usually just preoccupied with their own developmental or intellectual goals and forget about the goals of their parents.

Probably the most important parenting tip for keeping that adorable, precious infant as an adorable and precious child is to share fun and interests together. The more you share the positives, the fewer negatives you will experience. The more you have shared laughter and the magic of learning together, the more resilient your child will be during the negative periods in life. The positive relationships, the patterns, the guidelines, and the model you set will define the child you are proud of.

Perry McArthur Butterfield *was born in Denver, Colorado, and received a B.A. in American studies and sociology from Smith College and an M.A. in developmental psychology and counseling from the University of Colorado at Denver. She has also earned certification in probation counseling and in neonatal behavior assessment.*

Perry is a research psychologist, consulting on emotional development in children and on parenting issues, and is senior research associate in the Department of Psychiatry at the University of Colorado. For almost thirty years she has conducted research on the newborn infant and on parent-infant relationships and has published scores of articles. Among many public service projects in Colorado, she has helped design the new infant-toddler wing for the Denver Children's Museum and has served on Governor's task forces on parenting issues. She has three grown children.

If you bungle raising your children,
I don't think whatever else you do well
matters very much.

—JACQUELINE KENNEDY ONASSIS

Robert Kleemeier

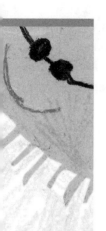

Childhood
Is Not a Disease

Many advances have been made in the *treatment and education* of troubled children during the more than a quarter of a century that I have been a practicing child psychologist.

More effective psychosocial and medication therapies are available, schools offer programs for students with disabilities, and abusive psychiatric hospitals have all but disappeared. But some troubling trends are emerging in the treatment and education of children.

Childhood is not a disease. Most children I see do not have diseases. They may be failing in school, fighting with parents, unable to sit still or pay attention for extended periods, and complaining of being unhappy, but they are not sick. What most children suffer from is an inability to get their needs met in the social and physical environments that they inhabit. When high-energy children are forced to sit for extended periods, when teachers don't teach, or when children lacking in academic intelligence are forced into college prep programs, there is bound to be trouble. They fight back, find ways to distract themselves, worry, and ultimately give up. True, some individuals do have damaged nervous systems that require fixing, but the vast majority do not.

> *America has developed a one-size-fits-all educational system despite the fact that children vary greatly in intelligence, interests, and temperament.*

Because clinicians have acquiesced to the insurance industry's policy of only paying for treating mental illnesses, children with the difficulties mentioned above end up being diagnosed with oppositional defiant disorder, attention deficit hyperactivity disorder, overanxious disorder of childhood, and depression. Aside from the stigma resulting from labeling environmental and developmental problems as illnesses, this diagnostic mania has led to the conclusion that children who don't fit in with their surroundings are either sick or bad. If sick they must be treated and if bad they must be punished. To parents, I offer the following observations and suggestions.

Most often it is the environment and not the child that is sick. The wise person changes the environment to fit the child's needs before trying to change the child. In my experience, the most dramatic improvements in children's behavior and feelings have come from placing them in schools or classes that meet their needs and from parents modifying their approaches to parenting. These improvements are

more immediate, profound, and long lasting than anything produced by individual psychosocial therapies, medication, or the juvenile justice system. The professional community has done the youth of this country a great disservice by describing the problems caused by absent and overstressed parents, disintegrating neighborhoods, poor teaching, crowded classrooms, boring lessons, and undiagnosed learning disabilities as childhood illnesses. These misdiagnoses have allowed society to avoid addressing the daunting task of reforming the institutions responsible for rearing children and instead have forced children to shoulder the blame.

A very positive consequence of the Americans with Disabilities Act has been to focus attention on ways that schools, homes, and other settings can be modified to accommodate those whose abilities fall outside of what is considered normal. Parents and teachers who perceive their children as having diseases react passively and let the doctors work a cure, but parents and teachers who approach each problem as a poor match between child and environment are empowered and devise some remarkably ingenious accommodations. The *hyperactive* primary student who attends a school with several daily recess periods and interactive learning centers can focus his or her excess energy on productive goals. The severely *dyslexic* middle schooler who has ready access to recorded books and computer screen readers can keep up with the rest of the class. And the *oppositional defiant disordered* teen who leaves a college prep program for a state-of-the-art vocational curriculum can be transformed from a sullen delinquent to a productive member of society.

What's a parent to do? Beyond becoming an environmental engineer, there are several things that I have found helpful in working with children and their parents.

Parents need to set reasonable expectations. Psychologists have put too much emphasis on teaching parents techniques for changing children and too little emphasis on considering why and if the child should be changed. Everyone benefits if it is accepted that individual differences exist, are good, and are not diseases. America has developed a one-size-fits-all educational system despite the fact that children vary greatly in intelligence, interests, and temperament. It is not surprising that parents have bought into this structure and think of their children as either college bound or

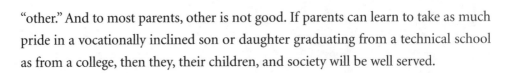

"other." And to most parents, other is not good. If parents can learn to take as much pride in a vocationally inclined son or daughter graduating from a technical school as from a college, then they, their children, and society will be well served.

An accurate diagnosis leads to appropriate help. Working with psychologists to help children discover their strengths and weaknesses is the first step in meeting children's needs, and one that is usually welcomed by the entire family. Children are genetically programmed to bond with parents, learn, and join the larger society. When this does not happen, it is because the child is being forced to do something that he or she does not have the ability for, interest in, or temperament for. Seek a clinician who begins with a comprehensive evaluation of both the child *and the environment* to serve as the basis for an intervention plan. This diagnostic role is most often filled by psychologists, while paraprofessionals or technicians provide the support.

Identifying what is troubling your child, being willing to change the elements in the environment that might be causing the problem, setting reasonable expectations of your child, and obtaining skilled assistance in diagnosing and treating any more serious problems will provide the help and support that your child needs to flourish.

Robert Kleemeier *hails from California but moved steadily eastward throughout his life. He received a B.A. from DePauw University in 1966 and a Ph.D. in psychology from Purdue University in 1971. For more than thirty years he has been a pediatric clinical psychologist. He and his wife, Carol, live outside of Atlanta.*

Children need love, especially
when they do not deserve it.

—HAROLD S. HUBERT

Sherleen Sisney

Relationships with Teachers

After ten years as a professional educator, I thought I knew the qualities of a successful teacher. Then I became a parent. I vividly recall a comment made by a student's parent shortly after my daughter's birth: "Now you will be a better teacher." It was true.

It has taken me twenty years of being both a parent and an educator to fully understand the meaning of that statement. I thought that I had always cared about the welfare of my students, and in many important ways I had. Yet the immediate impact of my becoming a parent was to magnify that concern because I realized that every student was as special to his or her parents as our daughter was to my husband and me. More than ever, I began to see the teacher and parent roles as seamless.

Decisions about where and how you educate your children are among the most important and difficult parenting decisions. With increasing opportunities for school choice, parents frequently ask me for advice about schools. After getting some information about their child and discussing the attributes of various schools and programs, my bottomline answer is always, "Whatever school you choose, all that really matters will be the relationships the student establishes, especially with a teacher or teachers in that school." Speaking as a teacher and a parent, if I could design the ideal environment for educating students, it would be based upon the philosophy that *relationships are primary.*

It is a very powerful thing when a teacher creates and nurtures a relationship with a student that *instills self-confidence, fosters a love of learning,* and *promotes a sense of community.* Clearly, good teachers leave their mark.

With amazing frequency, successful individuals who are asked to identify major influences in their lives quickly recall a favorite teacher. Almost without exception, that influence stemmed from the teacher's ability to establish a sense of self-worth that formed the foundation for the individual's successes. President Ronald Reagan echoed the feelings of many other highly accomplished individuals when he said it was a teacher "who first instilled in me a belief in myself."

Favorite teachers also are often credited with instilling a passion for some field of study or generating a lifelong love of learning. Again, this guidance must begin with the ability to establish a personal teacher-student relationship, and it is that relationship that is so often recalled with fondness and gratitude when people are asked about their favorite or best teacher.

A personal relationship with a teacher also helps the student feel connected to a community. The dynamics of the teacher-student relationship cannot operate in a vacuum but must expand into the wider community and, ultimately, throughout the student's life. Often an individual's success results from an ability to relate talent and motivation to the community at large. A successful teacher shows students the importance of connecting with the community and making a contribution to it.

Therefore I urge you to focus on your children's relationships with their teachers. Choose teachers noted for developing positive student-teacher relationships when a choice is available, and foster those relationships to the greatest extent possible.

Seek teachers who recognize and accept each child as an individual with a unique set of skills, abilities, and personality traits. Look for teachers who emphasize the critical nature of relationships, the search for knowledge, and the importance of communities. First look for schools and or programs with this philosophy; then identify individual teachers who embody it.

Relationships based on these principles are more likely to develop during a child's early years in school. By high school the promise of a personal relationship between student and teacher has been all but lost in the more detached, businesslike approach heralded as preparing the student for life. But such an environment robs teenagers of understanding at the most fundamental level and parents should continue to be involved in finding teachers who reach students on that personal level. My experiences as both an educator and parent leave me with no doubt that an affirmative, meaningful relationship between student and teacher can help young people believe

66...A lack of community or sense of belonging has created violence and victims in some of our high schools.99

in their ability to effect positive change. If that personal relationship exists, the teacher can teach anything. In truth, the material that the teacher presents takes on less importance because the framework that enables the student to relate to the learning process has already been established.

Helping young people learn to build relationships, connect with other people, and be accepted by them should be an integral part of formal education. High achievers often are alienated from the rest of the student body simply because they do excel academically. Underachieving students may be shunned because of their lack of academic success and its manifestations of acting-out behavior. Teachers can help all students learn to bridge the gaps that separate them. Help your children find teachers who direct programs and school activities that build a sense of community.

Loving a child doesn't mean giving in to all his whims;
to love him is to bring out the best in him,
to teach him to love what is difficult.

—NADIA BOULANGER

This sense of community, which is new to some students, is analogous to a family unit. Students discover that they are not so unusual after all and that "it's okay to be me." Such an atmosphere encourages each student to invest personally in the learning community and helps make it possible to develop a love of learning. All of us are painfully aware of how a lack of community or sense of belonging has created violence and victims in some of our high schools.

In recent years, much discussion has centered on what is not working in today's educational system. When attention is focused on what is working, we invariably see an emphasis on the development of personal and academic relationships. Often, too much importance is placed on tangible tools for generating student success, such as materials, textbooks, disciplinary codes, subject matter, and schedules. Don't be distracted from the underlying key to your children's ultimate happiness and success. As the plaque on my desk reminds me daily, "Relationships are Primary."

Sherleen Sisney *was born and raised in Stillwater, Oklahoma. She obtained her bachelor's degree in secondary education from the University of Oklahoma in 1968 and her master's degree in education from the University of Louisville in 1974. She is executive director of the Governor's Scholars program in Kentucky and works with at-risk adolescents in the Effective Learning program at Ballard High School in Louisville, where she taught social studies courses for over twenty years. In 1984 she was named the National Teacher of the Year. Sherleen and her husband, Lee, have one daughter, who is a college student.*

Michael R. Papciak

Behavior and Discipline

From the time their children are infants *until the adolescent years,* parents have many questions about the complexities of child rearing. Because every child's personalityand every family's characteristics are different, it can be difficult for parents to find specific information and practical answers that apply to their own everyday situations. But advice on these matters abounds.

Bookstores and libraries have shelves of books on parenting; television and newspapers offer a wide array of columnists who speak about child rearing issues; and now the Internet provides a multitude of web sites filled with information about raising children. None of these sources, however, is as useful as guidance from another parent or a childcare professional who knows your child. The wide range of parental concerns includes disrespectful behavior, temper tantrums, sleeping patterns, eating problems, toilet training difficulties, attentional or learning problems, and raising teenagers. As a doctor and the father of five children, I have found the following recommendations to be helpful for parents of children of all ages.

> 66 *Parents must hurt their child's feelings at times to influence or change behavior.* 99

ESTABLISHING LIMITS

Discipline is teaching limits to your child. The caring and love a parent feels for a child and the security a child experiences in the family make teaching rules and respect possible without adverse psychological consequences. Parents must hurt their child's feelings at times to influence or change behavior.

Both parents should agree on discipline rules, follow through on threats, and act consistently on a day-to-day basis with no exceptions. This approach must be followed by anyone else who takes care of your child, such as a relative, babysitter, or childcare provider.

Expect the same behavior from your children in public as you do at home; however, do not expect their best behavior when they are hungry or tired. An afternoon rest time or nap is necessary for most young children and all infants. Make sure your children do things on your terms. Do not change your behavior to suit their wishes. If they are demanding something right now, make them wait, even if only for a few minutes.

Teach children that the grownups are in charge in your home. Try to replace telling them that they are "good" or "bad" in certain situations by telling them instead that their actions or behavior "made Mommy and Daddy very happy (or unhappy)." It is easier to train young children to seek parental approval than it is to have them constantly frustrated as they try to control their own efforts. Let them think, "How can I make Mommy pleased or happy?" throughout the day's

activities. Children who grow up knowing they can walk all over their parents will have little or no respect for them.

Encourage your children and help them attain a good self-image, but be realistic and do not overdo it. Most children adjust better and demand less if they do not think of themselves as the smartest, prettiest, or cutest child in the world. Excessive complimenting or criticizing of children rarely changes behavior for the better and will erode self-esteem later. It helps to create the right atmosphere if you never gossip or criticize other people (relatives, neighbors, teachers) in front of your children.

DISCIPLINE AND PUNISHMENT

Punishment reinforces discipline and should be reserved for dangerous, destructive, and disrespectful intentional actions by your child. Rarely will a child need to be punished before the age of fifteen months.

"Time-out" is probably the best and most effective method of punishment for young children. Time-out may be in any safe area—playpen, gated room, or closed-door room. The parent must have control over the place and duration of time-out. Two to five minutes per year of age is a good guideline.

Spankings may be an effective means of getting the message across to some children if other methods fail. Spankings should be administered at the time of the precipitating event so the child can learn from the experience. Spankings should be on the bottom and administered with the hand only. Spankings should never be painful but should show the child who is in charge.

Taking away privileges or prized possessions works very well for the older child—ages five and above. You must follow through on all warnings or contracts with a consequence. Be consistent with your punishment and do not wait for the other parent to come home. Never turn away from a child if he or she is remorseful after misbehaving and receiving punishment. If your child seems to be unaffected by any of the above methods and there is no deterrent to misbehavior in your home, you have reached a critical stage in the child's development of a permanent sense of right and wrong. Please discuss this with your pediatrician and figure something out together before the "roof falls in."

TEMPER TANTRUMS

Behavior such as temper tantrums, breath holding, head banging, and other

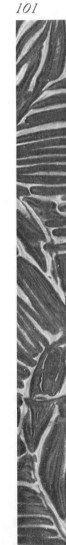

attention-getting tactics are normal in two- and three-year-old children. Such outbursts are best handled by putting the child off by himself or herself while trying to ignore the tantrum. This will take the child away from her audience. If the undesirable behavior is not upsetting anyone or commanding anyone's attention, it soon will stop. Reward your child's good behavior with your attention. It is important to follow this procedure both at home and in public places. If misbehavior occurs in public, stay calm and remind the child every three to five minutes on the way home that a punishment is coming and then follow through on the threat immediately when reaching home.

SLEEPING PATTERNS

All children, after the age of four months, should be expected to sleep eight to twelve hours each night if they are healthy. Most breast-fed infants may awaken during the middle of the night for a single feeding, and that time should be only for nursing. After the feeding, place the infant back in his or her bed and resume the nighttime sleep routine. Some preventive measures can help ensure that your child can easily get back to sleep after awakening during the night. One of the best is to put your baby to bed when awake rather than letting the infant be rocked, fed, or lulled to sleep in your arms or in bed.

Sleep is an important nutrient for the brain and will improve your child's behavior, attention span, and ability to learn. A full night's sleep for everyone in the family is essential for the child's proper growth and development and for the parents' survival. The happiest families are those with children who sleep in their own beds all night without interruption.

ADOLESCENCE

Building the bridges of communication between you and your adolescent begins many years before they reach their teens. Both parents should spend individual time with their children regularly from the time when they are very young. Strive for a natural friendship and trust with your child, but do not become a "pal." Encourage your child to read information about smoking, drug and alcohol abuse, sexuality, and sexually transmitted diseases, but remember that this is not a substitute for honest and frank discussions with you. If you are reluctant to talk to your children about these subjects, you cannot blame them for not involving you with their serious concerns later.

Children learn respect for members of the opposite sex, and other people in general, by parental example. Observing family relationships built around love, caring, and tenderness is the best way for children to learn about building long-lasting, respectful, and happy relationships with others.

During the past twenty-seven years of my pediatric practice, I have observed changes in parenting methods, in education, and in the environment in which children are raised. These changes have influenced the behavior, the attention spans, and the learning potential of many children. Because of these concerns, I give new parents the following advice in a handout. The results are amazing. Teaching certain parenting skills and changing the home-care environment early may help prevent future learning difficulties in some children. Consequently, educational achievement may be enhanced, family stress reduced, and the need for more drastic interventions such as medication eliminated.

TEN WAYS
TO IMPROVE LEARNING AND
PREVENT ATTENTIONAL PROBLEMS
IN CHILDREN

1. Touch and hold your child as much as possible in the first six months of life.

2. Limit television exposure until your child is twenty to twenty-four months of age. After age two restrict television to one hour per day, including computer time, videos, and video games. Never have a television set in a young child's room.

3. Encourage toys that stimulate the brain to work. Provide toys such as books, puzzles, blocks, stuffed animals, chalk, and crayons,

and eliminate those that merely provide sounds and words without requiring language use by the child.

4. Limit choices and reduce chaos by rotating toys in play areas or playrooms. With the exception of books, more is not better.

5. Promote independent play. Give young children fifteen or twenty minutes by themselves when they awaken from sleep. Encourage make-believe self-play when they get older.

6. Encourage activities that stimulate verbal interaction with parents or caretakers. Play interactive games that children enjoy such as London Bridge and Ring Around the Rosie. Talk with your children during grocery shopping, bath time, and family meals.

7. Provide physical limits to overactivity by using a playpen, defined play area, gates, or Dutch doors.

8. Beginning at birth, include thirty minutes of nonverbal, soft music in your child's routine each day. Continue this practice as long as possible. Sing to your child often.

9. Do not allow your child's sleep to be interrupted by other activities. This includes nighttimes, mornings, and nap times.

10. Instill sound dietary habits in your children. Provide balanced and nutritional meals. Eliminate most juices, sports drinks, and soft drinks between meals. Minimize exposure to excess sugar and additives.

Michael R. Papciak, *a graduate of the University of Michigan Medical School, has been a practicing pediatrician since 1974. He is past Chief of Pediatrics at Atlanta's Scottish Rite Children's Hospital and, in addition to his private practice, is now clinical assistant professor of pediatrics at Emory University School of Medicine. He is married and is the father of five children.*

Coleen C. Salley

Single Parenting: Not a One-Man (or Woman) Job

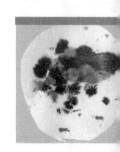

When I was twenty-five years old, I was sure I knew more about child rearing than my three brothers and sister, all of whom had children. Six years later when I was a widow with three children under the age of four, I realized I knew nothing!

My husband was in his last year of residency in Virginia when he died, and we were as poor as church mice. But I had two aces in the hole: an education and a pair of devoted grandparents.

The children and I lived with their grandparents for two years in Louisiana while I completed a master's degree. After graduation I accepted a position at a small college in South Carolina, against the wishes of my parents, siblings, and friends. But I had to find out if

I could handle being a single parent. As much as I needed and appreciated help, I felt that my children needed to know who was the final authority in their lives. I knew if I couldn't make it on my own I could always return to my parents. But I had to try. As it turned out, I never had to go back.

In the early years of single parenthood I read everything I could lay my hands on, with the result that I became so unsure of myself I couldn't make a decision about the simplest choices. Fortunately I decided to ditch the experts and embark on my own, because I never could have made it otherwise. Who has time to weigh every word or act? I loved my children, so I trusted myself to do what seemed right at the moment and, if possible, to rectify the mistakes later. Much later I told my grown children that although I may have made errors in judgment through the years, all my actions were motivated by love. Right or wrong, love was always present.

Let's begin in early childhood, the primary ages, those wondrous years when all behavior seems excusable. Enjoy them while they last. But believe me, you will enjoy them even more, especially as a single parent, if you establish routines, schedules, and firm limits—all of which help give your children a sense of security—that reflect your needs as well as those of your children.

Set limits for your children. Teach them at home that they are not the center of the universe. When George, my oldest, was about five, we went to a friend's house for dinner. As I was sipping a cocktail, George came over and asked for the cherry from my drink. "No," I told him. "When you're old enough, you may have your own drink with a cherry." He responded with a satisfied "Okay," and went back to play with the other kids. "I didn't know you could do that!" my friend exclaimed. "I've been giving up the cherry from my drinks for years!" (She had five children!) Hearing the word "no" is a part of life. Do not be afraid to say it to your children.

Establish routines. Every household, whether single parent or not, needs to set aside quiet times together, bonding times. One of my favorites is reading-aloud-together time. The American Booksellers Association has a program called Take Twenty. In-depth studies have proven that reading to children only twenty minutes a day makes a dramatic difference in their development. The Association is encouraging pediatricians to promote Take Twenty to parents.

Admit mistakes and apologize. Teach your children early to say "I'm sorry." You may hear yourself saying that phrase frequently in your early stages of parenthood. You will, or *should*, hear it more from them during the formidable teenage years. And for heaven's sake, don't hold grudges; children don't.

> ❝...*don't hold grudges; children don't.* ❞

Find a balance between encouraging and pushing your kids. I never felt completely comfortable with evaluating their performances in school. Was I demanding too much or not enough? When does encouraging become nagging? In the sixties and seventies, the world was so crazy, with old standards changing so rapidly, some disappearing altogether, that I was afraid to pressure my children too much. I wanted them to do their best, to realize their full potential, but what did that mean? Looking back I think I could have pushed the two boys more, but I was so busy pushing myself professionally that I didn't have enough energy left over to push them. Dinner still had to be cooked, homework checked, clothes washed, bills paid. Although I wasn't consistent about pushing them, I was always careful to compliment all three of my kids on their accomplishments. I remembered my father's warning, "Never tell a child he's bad, because then he'll have to live up to his reputation." Since my children all earned advanced degrees, I suppose the pressure applied was balanced enough, but I always wondered at the time.

Persevere through adolescence. Except for the two years after my husband's death, the years from ages thirteen to eighteen (a total of eight consecutive years for me) were the most harrowing. It was three against one! I was stupid and totally out of the mainstream, while their peers were wise and all knowing. Even my daughter, who had been the perfect child, became surly, argumentative, and secretive. One evening at dinner when all three kamikaze fighters were attacking, I told them, "Listen, I *love* you because I'm your mother, and I remember what dear, sweet children you used to be, but quite frankly I don't *like* any of you right now and would never choose one of you to be my friend!" But with a little effort and a lot of humor you can all survive those turbulent years.

Don't try to be "friends" with your children. They have enough friends; they need a parent.

Don't expect total honesty from your teenagers. I'm reminded of the old folk tale retold by Julius Lester. A farmer once saved a snake from freezing. The snake repaid the good deed by biting the farmer. When the farmer protested that the snake had promised not to bite him, the snake replied, "It is in the nature of a snake to bite. You knew that when you picked me up." My twist on that moral is: it is in the nature of teenagers to lie to parents. They'll do it no matter how good you are to them.

Maintain your authority. When my oldest child protested against one of my rules by declaring, "Well, you do it," my favorite rebuttal went like this: "Yes, I do. And I do lots of other things too. I pay the rent, buy you clothes, provide a phone for you to use, chauffeur you around, and feed you. I tell you what—let's do it like the government does. You come up with matching funds, and we'll be equals. You can do anything I do. But until that time you are *not* my equal. As the Army teaches: rank has privileges!" None of the three questioned my authority again.

Finally, I believe humor, spontaneity, and flexibility must play a role in any stage of child rearing, a really *big* role. Another sage adage of my father was "Every good rule must have an exception." Be flexible. Do the best you know how, and learn to laugh when things don't go as you expected. One day when your children are grown, paying rent, and raising kids of their own, then they will be your equals and will become the best friends you have ever had!

Coleen C. Salley *is a native of Ruston, Louisiana. She received her bachelor's and master's degrees from Louisiana State University and served as a teacher and librarian for over fifty years. She has written articles on effective ways to nurture and maintain children's natural curiosity about the world and was given the Distinguished Faculty award at LSU and the Outstanding Librarian award in Louisiana. Coleen currently is Professor Emeritus of Children's Literature at the University of New Orleans and travels widely, presenting in-service programs for educators and pursuing her other area of expertise, storytelling. She raised three children.*

We find a delight in the beauty and
happiness of children that makes
the heart too big for the body.

—RALPH WALDO EMERSON
The Conduct of Life

Gertrude F. Krick

The Building Blocks of Education

It is generally believed that education begins *at the school door.* Nothing could be farther from the truth. Most children begin their school experience with a background of learning that is truly impressive. Before they enter school they have mastered control of their bodily functions, they can feed themselves, use toys as a means of self-amusement, interact with peers and authority figures, and understand and accept limits on behavior. But most importantly, they have learned to use language as a means of communication.

From the moment a child is born, parents must take on the enormous responsibility of building this essential foundation upon which formal school teachings can be based.

Teaching, they say, is as much an art as it is a science. Parenting may be *more* art than science. Nevertheless, the art of teaching has much in common with parenting. Teachers must be thoroughly grounded in the subject matter they teach and in methods of teaching. But to be truly effective, they must feel free to try creative approaches and to make students a partner in the planning process. The art of teaching consists of capturing children's imaginations, finding keys to motivate them, and coming up with ways to involve them in the learning and teaching process. The art of parenting calls for these same skills.

If you plan to become a parent or if you are in the midst of raising a child, consider these pointers that I have gathered from my thirty-odd years as an elementary school teacher and administrator.

Learn to walk in your child's shoes, to see the world from your child's point of view. We cannot hope to reach our children if we fail to see things through their eyes. Observing a child's behavior from an adult point of view gives an incomplete picture. Sometimes it takes extra effort to find out what a child is seeing and feeling.

> Regina was a quiet little five-year-old. She was well behaved and gave no trouble in the classroom. She never volunteered information, did not interact with other children, and rarely chose a toy to play with or a book to read. Most of the time, she sat silently and observed what was going on around her.
>
> Troubled, her teacher invited Regina's mother for a conference and asked, "What does Regina tell you about her time in school?"
>
> "Oh," the parent replied, "she loves school. She comes home every day very enthusiastic!" She then recited a detailed description of all the activities of a typical school day.
>
> Obviously, a lot more was going on in Regina's head than appearances had indicated. Gradually, mother and teacher made efforts to involve the girl with hands-on activities and to foster social interaction. In time, she began to participate in classroom routines.

One day, as Regina was building a structure with blocks, the teacher said, "What an interesting building! Tell me about it."

"Oh," Regina replied, "this is Noah's Ark, this is his family, and these are the animals going into the ark two by two so they won't drown."

The teacher had read the story of Noah to the class three months earlier. Intrigued, she asked, "What made you decide to build Noah's Ark today?"

Regina looked up, plainly surprised at the question, and replied, "Don't you see how hard it is raining today?"

When you think you perceive a problem in your child, try to see the world through his eyes. Sometimes we adults forget that each child is unique and that each child sees the things around him and learns about them in his own unique way.

Don't be afraid to go "outside the beaten path" when you attempt to get something across to your child. Creative approaches, of course, may or may not produce the desired results. All teachers have sometimes wondered whether our methodology will yield desired outcomes, particularly if the approach is unconventional. Have we gone overboard, giving students too much license to go it alone? Or have we set too many rules and restrictions, limiting our students' freedom to use their own imaginations and creativity? Parents face the same questions. But you as a parent will soon learn whether or not a certain approach is working. Over time you can discover the approaches that suit your child best just by observing the results. No teacher in his or her right mind would continue using a method that never produces the desired outcome. But the smart teacher will use again and again methods that have proved to be successful. It doesn't make sense for you as a parent to pay any less attention to your approaches to raising your child.

A teacher divided his fifth-grade class into groups studying the geography and culture of various regions of the U.S. The teacher announced a two-part exam, but explained to the students that they would not be graded and did not need to study for the exam. The teacher merely wanted to evaluate the team approach.

Students were asked to think of themselves as a member of a chamber of commerce and respond to a request for information about a state they were studying, a request from an imaginary family that was considering relocating to that state. In the first part of the test, the students were to describe that state in such a way as to encourage the family to move there. The results were outstanding. When the teacher announced the next day that there would be no need for the second half of the test, the class chorused: "But you promised!" They completed the second half of the exam—equally well. Having an entire class ask for a test was a first.

If your children see the purpose for what they are learning and if they are having a good time while learning, your approach is working. If not, try another approach.

> **❝If your children see the purpose for what they are learning...your approach is working.❞**

Recognize your child's fears, but keep them in proportion. Most teachers at one time or another have encountered a young child who is traumatized by so-called school phobia—anxiety, timidity, fear associated with attending a class or going to school. This poses problems not only for the child, but also for parents, teachers, and administrators. Often the child cannot identify or articulate the cause of his or her malaise. Instead, the problem is manifested by physical ailment, distress, and a desire to go home. The teacher cannot be expected to cope with a crying, sick child, so administration must step in to try to cope with the problem.

Michael had just transferred from a private kindergarten to our school. He was an "outsider" and very unhappy. He cried daily in class, distracting teacher and students alike. He was finally sent to administration. The following conversation ensued:

"Michael. I know you're feeling bad," said Mrs. Bailey. "You miss your kindergarten teacher and friends, don't you? Be patient. You'll make friends here too, and soon you'll begin to feel comfortable. When you cry in class, the teacher can't teach and the children can't learn."

"I have to cry," said Michael. "My stomach hurts and I want to go home."

"You're right, Michael," Mrs. Bailey said. "You do have to cry. You can cry for fifteen minutes."

"I need more time than that!" Michael cried.

"In this school you're allowed to cry for fifteen minutes," Mrs. Bailey answered. "Can you tell time?"

"No."

Mrs. Bailey took off her wristwatch. "Look at this watch," she said. "When the little black stick moves to this number you'll know that fifteen minutes are up."

Michael took the watch, stopped crying, and focused his attention on the minute hand as it moved to the designated number. He then returned the watch.

"You're a gentleman and a scholar, Michael," said Mrs. Bailey, giving Michael a hug and a kiss. "Now you may return to class."

Michael did so, without crying. He was not sent out of class again, ultimately made new friends, and adjusted well to his class.

Of course, not all problems are solved that easily, but this is a good example of a creative approach to dealing with a child's fears. Parents, like teachers, need to find ways to show children that they understand their fears while helping them keep their fears in proportion.

The analogy between parents and teachers does break down after a point. After all, the parent must play the role of the administrator as well as that of the teacher. The parent cannot appeal to some higher authority when problems arise. Nevertheless, the point is the same for teachers, for school administrators, and for parents. Children need understanding and reassurance from time to time, but they also need guidance and limits. Acknowledge and empathize with your child's pain and fear. Offer your child opportunities to vent. And once you have decided on a course of action, gently insist that the child stay the course.

Parenting, like teaching, can be a tremendously rewarding and at times a tremendously frustrating undertaking. One who is dedicated to working with children

must be prepared to cope with both ends of the continuum—and everything in between. But there is no denying that the rewards make it all worthwhile.

Gertrude F. Krick *was born in New York City. She received a B.A. from Hunter College in 1934, an M.A. in early childhood development from Teachers College of Columbia University in 1936, and thirty years later an M.A. in reading from Emory University. For many years she taught at Emory University and at the Hebrew Academy of Atlanta, where she also served as assistant principal. She received the Woman of Achievement award in Atlanta. Gertrude and her husband, Edward, have two children and a bunch of grandchildren and are extremely active in the community.*

116

[Growing up] is especially difficult to achieve for a child whose parents do not take him seriously; that is, who do not expect proper behavior from him, do not discipline him, and finally, do not respect him enough to tell him the truth.

—THOMAS S. SZASZ
National Review

Thomas C. Johnson

The Gift
of a
Healthy Lifestyle

*O*ne *of the major purposes* of the sports *fitness camp that I direct* is to promote an appreciation of physical activity by providing an environment for boys and girls in which exercise is both challenging and enjoyable. During my three decades of supervising and watching children as they grow through their experiences in the summer camp, I have come up with a few recommendations to offer to parents who are starting out on a lifetime of child rearing.

Begin early to encourage your child to lead a healthy lifestyle. All parents should recognize the importance of healthy lifestyles and the need for their children to be physically active early in life. I firmly believe that positive physical fitness and sports experiences during a child's formative years not only will result in immediate benefits but also will encourage continued participation in healthy physical activities throughout adulthood.

When your children are very young, provide them with activities that encourage the development of motor skills. Before children can begin to develop complex movement skills as they mature, a foundation of basic motor skills must be established. Without the basic movement skills, children are often placed in uncomfortable and threatening situations and develop an aversion to physical activity. Establishing and building on basic motor skills is essential if children are to participate in and enjoy physical activity.

Provide your child with a positive learning environment. Create and maintain a nurturing, noncompetitive environment that encourages youngsters as they acquire and develop basic skills, perform a variety of fitness-oriented activities, and interact with peers.

Establish realistic expectations for your child. Remember that each child is unique as far as motor skills, physical fitness, abilities, interests, and experiences are concerned. A physical activity that allows for wide variation in individual performance and differences in each child's capabilities—an activity that does not impose group expectations and standards—works best for most children.

Help your child find activities that are physically demanding, fun, and challenging. Studies have shown that the youth of our country are physically unfit and are becoming increasingly obese. In short, they are products of the society in which they live. Lifestyles that encourage physical inactivity, excessive TV viewing, an obsession with video games or computers, and unhealthy nutritional habits contribute to the generally unfit status of children. If your child's school does not have a quality physical education program, search your community for a good program with a diverse offering of physical activities that develop motor skills, increase physical fitness, and encourage an appreciation for active lifestyles.

From time to time, expose your child to a structured environment and rigorous discipline. I am convinced that it is in such a setting that a child can best acquire skills, improve performance, attain a sense of achievement, learn respect for others, and establish positive personal interactions. Structure and discipline do not inhibit creativity and individuality; they can often encourage the expression of these traits.

Emphasize participation, not performance. Once your child is engaged in a sport or physical program, expect and encourage him or her to try, to participate, to be a part of all activities. The level of performance is not as important as enthusiastic, energetic participation.

Seek out activities for your child that will help develop confidence. Peers often ridicule other children for their lack of physical and motor skills and accomplishments. Find a program or activity that tries to provide equal participation for each child, a minimum of criticism, and a feeling that each child, regardless of ability, can contribute to the success of the team. You are trying to encourage, not discourage, your child to participate in physical activities, so it is important to look for the most positive atmosphere possible.

Don't try to administer self-esteem to your children. I don't believe that self-esteem can be packaged and dispensed. Children develop confidence and subsequently a sense of self-esteem when they believe in themselves, accomplish a task whether it is physical or cognitive, achieve a goal, and in the process realize that they have the character and ability necessary to perform at a certain level. In short, children need to feel good about themselves, and it is our responsibility as parents to help them establish realistic goals and to provide quality instruction, reinforcement, and encouragement.

Encourage your children to give their best effort, and discourage them from quitting. I am convinced that failure is not necessarily bad, especially if an effort is given and the appropriate analysis and reinforcement are provided. Failure can open the door to growth in character and commitment. I believe that parents should not tolerate quitting or giving less than the best effort possible, and that they should encourage their children to try. Parents have to discover the delicate balance between the merits of allowing children to fail in certain tasks with the anticipation of further growth and temporarily "saving" them by saying it's okay to avoid the challenge or quit the task. In sports and games, for example, it is important to teach your child that the inability to finish first does not always mean that he or she is inferior or is a failure. Our society overemphasizes the significance of being first; we often ignore the intrinsic value of participating and giving one's best. Help your child maintain a wholesome perspective as far as winning, losing, and participating are concerned.

Be consistent when it comes to expectations, rewards, and punishments. Impress on your child the fact that he or she is responsible for his or her actions, and that certain actions will result in negative consequences.

Participating in organized physical activities not only improves children's fitness and motor skills but also builds their self-confidence. While developing new skills and practicing techniques, children enjoy themselves and acquire an appreciation for physical activity that will help them become healthier adults. What a wonderful gift for any parent to give a child!

Thomas C. Johnson *received his bachelor's degree from Mercer University, a master's in education from Emory University, and a doctorate in education from the University of Georgia. He is currently Professor of Physical Education at Emory University, where he has been on the faculty for more than thirty-five years. For over a generation, he has been director of the Emory Sports Fitness Camp for children. He is the author of numerous articles dealing with youth soccer and children's fitness. Tom is a member of the Emory University Sports Hall of Fame and was NCAA Coach of the Year in 1984. An athlete and research scholar, Tom is an avid tennis player and amateur Civil War historian. He and his wife, Kay (also a contributor to this volume), have two children and two granddaughters, and they are now looking forward to their first grandson.*

Henry Harsch

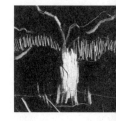

Raising Boys

If people were required to read a full job *description* of parenting before taking it on, many of them would change their minds and back out. If they still wanted the job, however, the first question I would ask them would be, "Do you really like children?" If they answered "No," or even "They're okay," I would strongly recommend that the applicant stay away from parenting. This job can be immensely rewarding, but it can be an overwhelming responsibility. It calls for hard work, long hours, and complete dedication, as well as continual on-the-job learning and training.

As demanding a job as child rearing is, raising boys offers its own special challenges. While I realize that most advice about raising a son can apply equally to raising a daughter, I would like to address several issues from the boy's standpoint.

DEVELOPING COMPETENCIES

Boys are a complex package. Their energy and exuberance can sometimes be exhausting to parents. From an early age, boys want to do things for themselves. They will put a great deal of effort into developing skills that are important to them, often spending hours making things or doing things on their own. Helping and supporting boys as they develop competencies can be tricky. Good parents keep trying until they discover how to walk that fine line between too little and too much help. They try to avoid doing something for their children that they can do for themselves.

This also applies to developing competencies in communications and relationship skills. One of our boys received

Our children may learn about the heroes of the past. Our task is to make ourselves architects of the future.

—JOMO MZEE KENYATTA

a lower mark on an English paper because he had included a fact that he had found in the encyclopedia rather than in the class text. He felt very strongly that he shouldn't be penalized when his motivation for going beyond the text had been to learn more. We encouraged him to talk to the teacher about the matter, but he said he was scared and wanted us to do it. We told our son we would be willing to talk to his teacher as a last resort, but then we encouraged him to do it himself. Finally the three of us scheduled a conference with the teacher. We let our son do the talking, but we let him know that we were there to back him up if he needed it. The teacher listened, understood, agreed with him, changed the grade, and thanked him. Our son learned that he was competent to communicate in this situation, and he learned that we were available to back him up when necessary.

EXPRESSING FEELINGS

In my work with couples, I hear from female partners again and again that their male partners lack the ability to express feelings, find it hard to be intimate, and generally are not very available emotionally. According to Dr. William Pollack, who wrote REAL BOYS, "Researchers have found that at birth, male infants tend to be more emotionally expressive than female babies. But by the time boys reach elementary school much of their emotional expressiveness has been lost or it has gone underground."

Dr. Pollack faults a widely practiced child rearing custom for this phenomenon. Many parents fear that mothers will feminize their boys if they spend too much time with them or get too close to them emotionally. Mothers sometimes accept the notion that their presence, their influence, and their more freely expressed emotions are just not good for boys. Often parents share the worry that their boy might become too feminine, that he will be teased and taunted, and that he will not be able to establish his rightful place in the world of boys and men.

This fear has been so embedded in our culture that other people who have influence in the child's life—extended family members, physicians, teachers, ministers, and even psychologists—perpetuate the myths and customs that grow out of it. The truth is that a mother's presence and influence is crucial in a boy's life. The mother is often the main parental influence for nurturing the ability to care for others, to express feelings, to connect with others, and to be kind, responsible, and thoughtful.

TEAMWORK

It is my belief that good parenting is a team effort of commitment, communication, joy, and responsibility, with the children included as a valuable part of the team. Each member of the team shows a healthy respect, understanding, and appreciation of the others, recognizing and accepting their different styles or approaches.

When you are raising a child, try not to divide tasks along gender lines. Perhaps Dad has his own way to change a diaper. Mom may be much better at it, but if she insists that he do it her way, Dad feels inept and defers to Mom, letting her take over that task. It is easy to see how the job of parenting can become compartmentalized at an early stage. Avoid falling into this pattern and emphasize the team effort instead. Share freely in all parenting functions—from diaper

changing to bedtime storytelling, from disciplining to helping with homework—and work together as a team. When your children are old enough, allow them to join in, once again being careful not to divide tasks along gender lines.

THE "BOY CODE"

We have all heard the admonitions: Boys need to be tough. They must look and act strong, and they don't cry. Boys must not show feelings of doubt, of pain, or of sadness. Boys must not show tender feelings toward other boys or demonstrate qualities that some people consider to be feminine, such as being highly involved in schoolwork or participating in class discussions. Many adults and most of a boy's peers reinforce and intensify this kind of gender stereotyping, often referred to as the "boy code." By the time a young boy reaches school age, he is allowed only a narrow range of behaviors.

This masculine code of behavior developed when times called for tough men to fight wars and to pioneer new lands. Today the need is for a more collaborative man who can mediate with men and women and communicate with and be more emotionally available to his partner and his children. What we once discouraged in raising our sons is now exactly what we need to promote.

I feel that the boy code continues to dominate our culture because it is a defensive behavior that wards off some unconscious pain. The attitude and behaviors of remaining unattached, uninvolved, unfeeling, inexpressive, or "cool" serves to keep vulnerability at bay.

Unfortunately, boys taunting boys to enforce the boy code remains a part of the boy culture. Sometimes the boy code becomes a convenient mask for bullying. This type of cruel teasing destroys the victim's emotional esteem and self-confidence and creates in the taunted boy the perception that he is an outsider and that he can't look to his peers for help or support.

It is sad that often a boy who feels helpless to solve the problem on his own also feels that he can't look to his school or his parents for support either. He may see them as helpless, too. If your son is experiencing difficulties at the hands of a bully, you do not have to let the situation stand. You are not helpless. You can go to the school, not to complain, but rather to see if you can help with the problem. Consult with your son to see what ideas he has about the problem.

Discuss the problem with a trusted teacher or counselor.

LISTENING

Your son's decisions about sex, drinking, and drugs can have serious repercussions on his future. Do not wait to convey your values, your ideas, and pertinent information to your boy. Propose a time when the three of you can talk. Let your son know that you are willing to listen to him without being critical or judgmental. Even though you may hear some things you would rather not hear, allow your son to speak his mind without interruption. Give him a chance to speak his mind in a safe setting so that you can look at everyone's views fairly and honestly. If you actively and patiently listen to him, he will be more likely to listen to you as well. And everything can't be said in an evening. Keep meeting. The better the climate set at these meetings, the better the chances all of you will want to meet again.

SOME GUIDELINES FOR RAISING BOYS

■ Talk to boys in a way that honors their pride and masculinity.

■ Stay connected with your boy and become knowledgeable about his world.

■ Fathers, step up and get your sweet rewards by staying actively involved in parenting.

■ Encourage a full range of emotional expression, and provide complete and unconditional empathy and understanding for a full range of feelings.

■ Express your love and empathy openly, generously, and often.

■ Avoid the use of shaming language.

■ Do not laugh when a boy expresses vulnerable feelings. Laughing at him can turn the expression of vulnerability into a shaming experience.

■ Discourage taunting and teasing. Send a clear message that these behaviors are not okay and that there are better ways to express uncomfortable feelings.

■ Enlist your boy's help to look into aggressive behaviors and try to discover the driving forces behind them.

■ Acquaint yourself with the telltale signs of depression and suicide risk. If you see your boy showing these signs, get immediate professional care.

■ Build a family structure in which each member shares some authority.

■ Include boys and their sisters in an ongoing family dialogue about family problems and their solutions.

■ Help your boys and girls connect, and help them reconnect when a glitch occurs in the connection.

■ Encourage boy/girl friendships at all ages.

■ Create a model of masculinity that is broad and inclusive.

■ Encourage your boy in all of his gender and cross-gender interests and relationships.

■ Let your boy know that big guys do cry; let him know that you sometimes cry.

■ Give your boy opportunities to learn about or meet people who bend society's strict gender rules—male nurses, female plumbers, girls who are jocks, boys who cook.

■ Give your boy a sense that there are many ways to be manly.

■ Find a way to comfortably accept your boy's sexuality, including masturbation.

■ Let your boy know that no matter what he enjoys doing, who he likes spending time with, what sorts of feelings he experiences, he's a real boy and he's on his way to being a real man.

Henry Harsch *hails from Stanton, Nebraska. After receiving a Ph.D. in clinical psychology from the University of Georgia, he became a child psychologist and family psychotherapist and has served the community in that capacity for more than forty-four years. He and his wife, Jean, who is a licensed clinical social worker, have raised two daughters and four sons.*

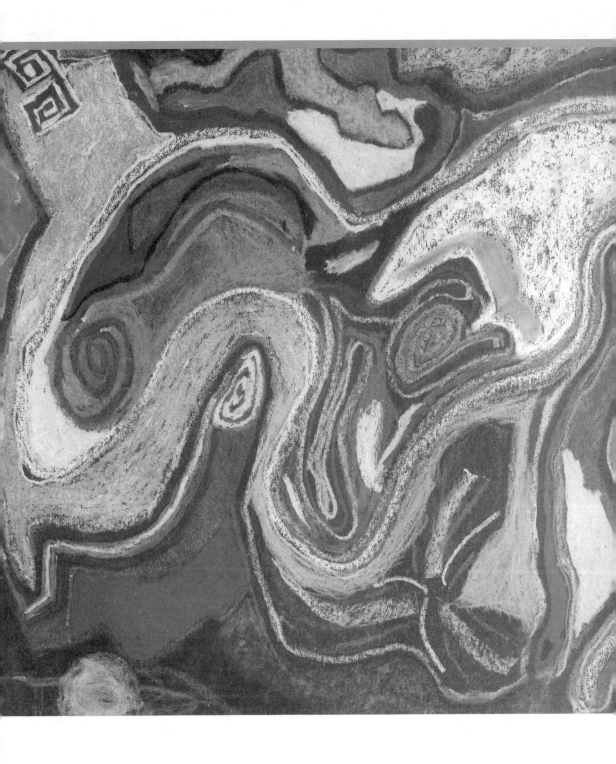

Carl A. Grant

Raising Children
in a World of Inequalities

As my children begin families of their own,
I often think about what advice I might offer to them—to all young
people who are facing the task of raising children of color in a society marked by race, class, and gender inequalities.

Parenting—being responsible for the care of a child—is an awesome responsibility. Both because of the continuous changes in society and because of the institutionalized traditions and attitudes of
people, parenting will probably be the most challenging teaching and
learning experience that you will ever undertake. Once you become a
parent, you will have very few, if any, vacation days from this responsibility. In fact, you'll have to keep even short breaks to a minimum,

especially when your children are very young or when they are adolescents. Yet in spite of the constant demands within the family and the pressures from outside the family, parenting is a rare privilege that ranks at the top of the list for human fulfillment.

Raising a child is one of life's great adventures. But before you embark on this adventure, learn as much as you can about yourself. If you feel self-assured and secure, it will help you to be fair and just with your children and to model the attitudes and behaviors that you want them to acquire. Displaying a confident attitude and demonstrating self-reliance will encourage your children to become independent persons, not "wannabe's" who are easily influenced by media and peer culture. My own mother and father shaped my belief in the importance of self-confidence. My brothers and I often talked about how Mom and Dad were not swayed by "what the Joneses did." They never allowed us to submit to peer pressure, rewarding us instead when we could show them that our reason for doing something was based on thoughts of our family or of our own future, rather than on immediate gratification or on keeping up with our friends.

Allow and encourage your children to become their own persons, to pursue life opportunities that can fulfill their dreams. If you feel positive about yourself, you will be able to love your children without demanding their love in return. If you are secure about yourself, you will be able to cut the apron strings—to acknowledge that while your children are a lifetime blessing, they are not yours to own.

Appreciate your children while they are under your care and enjoy the many roles you play with them. I recall when my two children left home for college. The house went from being as noisy and hectic as a zoo—the phone ringing constantly, their friends stopping by, the fridge rapidly going from full to empty, the constant churning of the washing machine and buzzing of the clothes dryer—to being as solemn and quiet as a library. During the time when the house was like a zoo, I yearned for peace and quiet. As soon as they left home, I missed their noise and energy.

Keep the lines of communication open and active and make certain that both your words and actions can be trusted. Learn when, where, and how to communicate with your children, and remember that sometimes the less said, the better. Allow your children to make their own decisions as often as possible so they will gain independence and confidence. Always keep in mind, however, that sometimes you will need to sit down with them and review the guidelines of responsibility.

Help your children learn who they are so during both life's dark times and its bright times they will remain true to themselves and live their life in a wholesome way. Teach your child that learning about oneself is a continuous venture. My family lived in England for a year. I remember the time when my son's middle school teacher and some of his student friends challenged him over the spelling of some words (centre for center; colour for color). He stood his ground and demanded that grade points not be deducted from his science project merely because he had used the American way of spelling. I asked if he wanted me to talk with the teacher, but he said that he would handle it—and he did. In that situation he learned that he could stand tall and speak up for himself even when those around him argued that he was wrong.

> **" *Teach them to understand that when they do a deed, good or bad, it affects all family members.* "**

133

Help your children understand and appreciate the importance of family. Let them know that within the family they always have a source of love and support, but at the same time be sure that they understand their duty and responsibility to other family members. Teach them to understand that when they do a deed, good or bad, it affects all family members.

Discuss all aspects of parenting with your spouse or with other caregivers. No matter what constitutes your family—whether you are a single parent or share parenting responsibilities with a partner, a spouse, or a member of the extended family—make sure that your children understand their relationship and responsibility to each individual within the family.

Inform your children, especially since they are children of color, about how some people in society may view them, and why they are sometime seen in a particular way. Help them to understand that life isn't always fair. Never let them, however, lose focus on the prizes they seek or give up because of the ignorance and narrowness of others. Teach them that many people strive to be fair and reasonable, and encourage them to judge people by their character and actions, not by some politically constructed social marker, such as race or socio-economic status. Make your daughter aware of gender stereotypes, inequities caused by sexism, and the importance of determination and perseverance while she pursues her life goals. Teach your son about the importance of equality and equity between males and females, especially in his personal relationships. Explain to him that although males and females are different, one gender should not dominate another, and that the barometer of success should not be based upon standards set by males. Teach both your girls and boys how to have a voice and to respond to unfair treatment whether directed at themselves or toward others.

When my children were growing up, I felt a strong responsibility to teach them about different perspectives and various groups of people. Schools and society at large are still greatly lacking in accepting and affirming diversity and attending to equity. See to it that your kids learn about peoples of different cultures and ethnicities. Help them to appreciate poetry, stories, plays, and music from other traditions as well as their own.

You must remain constantly vigilant about the treatment of your children in school. The African-American male is often unjustly the subject of false labeling and unfair practices, but young women sometimes face similar wrongs. I recall the times when people treated my daughter unjustly because she questioned the narrowness of the curriculum or requested the inclusion of works and histories of people of color. Your children will always need your help and encouragement, but there will also be times when you will need to visit your children's school to support them.

Take time to teach your children about the importance of the joys of life—a day at the ballpark, museum, or zoo; a quiet and peaceful moment together, even in a very noisy place; and the rare privilege of sharing time with a true friend.

Help your children appreciate the beauty and mystery of nature. Tell them that they have a responsibility to the global village in which they live.

Remind your children of the many people throughout the world who have not been blessed with material benefits and medical services, and help your children recognize that they have a responsibility to share and to make life better for others. Enable them to understand that equity and equality are not just for people living in the U.S. or for people within their own race, gender, and life-style group.

Finally I say to my own children, be yourself. You are kind, caring, and thoughtful human beings. I have every faith in you, and I believe that you will be excellent parents for your children. The knowledge and attitude that you have acquired thus far will help you be the parents you wish to be and the parents your children will love and respect.

135

Carl A. Grant *is currently Hoess-Bascom Professor in the Department of Curriculum and Instruction at the University of Wisconsin-Madison. He graduated from Tennessee State and earned his master's degree from Loyola University in Chicago. In 1972 he received his Ph.D. from the University of Wisconsin-Madison. He has been a teacher and an assistant principal in the Chicago Public School system. Carl is the father of two children and has one grandchild.*

Selective ignorance, a cornerstone of child rearing.
You don't put kids under surveillance; it might frighten you.
Parents should sit tall in the saddle and look upon their troops with
a noble and benevolent and extremely nearsighted gaze.

—GARRISON KEILLOR
Leaving Home

Judith Soloff Werlin

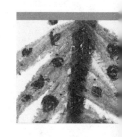

Providing Context
and Balance

𝒥have been a high school educator for thirty years. Every day I come to class determined to connect the student with the material more successfully than I did yesterday. The thought that I can engage my students in the passion of my life—teaching history—is what gets me up every morning willing— or almost willing—to navigate the snows of Wisconsin. Over the years I've reached the conclusion that my repertoire of historical spellbinders and my bag of skills rely on a few cardinal principles. The more I talk with children and with their parents, the more convinced I become that these principles can also work at home.

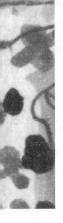

My passion for teaching history to young people reflects my passion for what I call the teaching process. History is a web of details—some tantalizing, some gruesome, some memorable, many forgettable. What are we to do with all the details? We need some principles to help us evaluate them. We also need a way of assigning them to the "right spots" on our internal map. Principles often vary in accord with generational differences, cultural bias, national identity, and other considerations. Some details deserve a prominent place in our memory; others are trivial.

So how do we learn to fit the details into the right spots? With all the information now available to us and to our children, how do we teach them to ask perceptive questions about it? How do we train them not to be overawed by the impressive media—like alluring web sites and slick magazine articles—that clamor for their attention? As a teacher of history, I try to give my students the skills to evaluate both the details and the media that present them.

As a parent you face a similar challenge. Your children are constantly exposed to information from radio, television, videos, and movies; from books, newspapers, and magazines; and now from the Internet. You must provide the context and the balance by which they can master this maze.

From the time your children are very young, you can help them begin to develop the critical thinking skills that I reinforce in my history classes.

Encourage the lively debate of ideas in your home.

Engage your children in conversation about the world and its issues.

Encourage them to ask questions about current events, and if you don't know the answers, help them find out where to look.

Keep reference books, maps, puzzles, and educational games readily available, urge your children to use them, and use them yourself.

If your kids see that you enjoy learning, they will want to join in. By the time they reach their high school history class, they will be on their way to becoming critical thinkers and intelligent consumers of information.

Try to avoid being judgmental about your child's abilities. As the school year progresses, it becomes harder and harder for me as a teacher not to categorize each student—this one is always late with assignments, this one is lazy, this one is confident—but I do my best to reevaluate their contributions every day. Many parents come to me with an image of their child that differs completely from the child I see in my classroom. Some have categorized their child and cannot see any changes in them. Others see in their child only what they want to see.

My advice to parents parallels my classroom philosophy. Believe in your child; be his advocate, but not his enabler. Don't try to reshape her in your image. Set clear standards and communicate them clearly, but give your child space to grow, to ask questions, to try out new ways of looking at issues. Don't be afraid that her values will suffer if you allow her to question your assumptions. Respect your child as an individual. A relationship—whether between parent and child or teacher and student—cannot be fruitful in the absence of mutual respect.

I work hard to create a climate of trust and safety in my classroom. I want my students to take risks intellectually while feeling emotionally safe. When the climate is right, students feel free to share their dreams, their questions, even their private thoughts about themselves. They are able to engage in lively debate and challenge each other's ideas without attacking each other's integrity. I try to maintain this atmosphere with a sense of humor. I give them time to express themselves, but I also set time limits. I give them some freedom in how they do their work, but I hold them accountable. I'm honest when I don't know the answer to a question or when someone raises a point I'd never considered. I emphasize civility and respect and avoid sarcasm and the witty put-down.

Children also need a climate of trust at home, especially when they reach adolescence. They need an atmosphere that invites them to share, to question, to debate, to explore new ideas, and to learn how to use freedom. They also need boundaries and examples of civil and respectful relationships. Members of a family must work and play in close proximity. Establish a pattern of civility and appreciation for one another. Never put your children down and do not tolerate put-downs from them.

> **"*Many parents come to me with an image of their child that differs completely from the child I see in my classroom.*"**

139

Prioritize your time and help your children schedule their time wisely. Don't allow them to overload their schedules so much that they leave themselves no time for fun and the building of relationships that foster trust and safety. The after-school job and the music lessons and the sports team as well as the AP courses can all seem great, but such a pace may be exhausting your child, making it impossible to enjoy family or school.

Don't let yourself be caught up in the minutiae of daily survival. Keep things in perspective; decide what is important and don't waste words or effort on the unimportant things. Cultivate the art of patience. Learn to recognize times when a smile or a laugh will defuse an uncomfortable situation. Let your children see your concern for others, especially for your spouse.

Children learn from role models, and usually the most important models in their lives are their parents. It can be a daunting task to be a role model for your child, but it can also be among the most satisfying of life's callings.

Judith Soloff Werlin *was born in Lakewood, New Jersey. She received her B.A. from Douglas College in 1966 and her M.A. from Teachers College at Columbia University in 1967. Judith has worked with teenagers in formal and informal settings for more than thirty years as a camp teacher and counselor and as a history teacher in junior high and senior high schools. She currently is chair of the History Department at Brookfield Academy in Wisconsin. She and her husband, Steven, who is a pediatric gastroenterologist, have two grown children. Judith also enjoys hiking, biking, and reading Hebrew literature.*

Stephen Nowicki Jr.

How to Make Friends

It was early Monday morning. As part of my responsibilities as a consultant, I was standing with a teacher and watching parents drop off their children for school. Blustery March winds made it feel even colder than the temperature on the thermometer. The children, bundled up against the weather, got out of their cars one after another, said their good-byes, and rushed off toward the school. As I continued to watch, a blue Honda Accord pulled up and stopped. A mother stepped out the driver-side door, walked around the car, and opened the passenger-side door for her daughter, an appealing girl about six years old. The little girl got out, and the two of them stood there looking at each other for a moment. Abruptly the mother said with a hint of command, "Go make friends now, Amy!" She patted her daughter on the head, walked back around the car, opened her door, got in, and drove off.

I still remember how forlorn Amy looked, almost lost in her large coat. She stood there with a bewildered expression on her face. Her mother had given her this seemingly simple assignment to "make friends." I could imagine Amy thinking, "How exactly do I do that?" After a time the little girl glanced around, slowly turned, and walked hesitantly toward the school.

If you were going to help Amy out, what would you tell her? How exactly do we go about "making friends"? This essential question is not as easy to answer as it first appears. However, when I think about what is really important for children to know and what is crucially important for adults to teach them, I can't think of anything more valuable than lessons in "how to make friends." Why is the answer to this question so important? Because a simple truth is that those who have the knack of making friends are most likely to be happy and satisfied, while those who bungle this task are probably destined to be unhappy and lonely.

Stop for a moment and take notice of the emotional "debris" all around you that comes from the failures—at both the adult and child levels—to "make friends." Does a day go by when you don't read some newspaper headline or hear some newscaster reporting about relationship abuse of one kind or another—husband against wife, mother or father against child, son or daughter against aged parent? Who among us has not seen the pain that results from divorce? Those who teach or work with children know better than most of us what a surprisingly large number of kids are shunned and rejected by their peers. More than anything else we want to belong and to be with others in relationship, and yet we fail at this task more times than we would like to admit.

It is ironic that we get continual formal education and guidance throughout our childhood in how to deal with words and numbers, but we get relatively little help when it comes to the crucially important skill of learning how to relate to people. Schools spend millions of dollars to develop academic programs and standardized multiple-choice tests to evaluate them while providing next to nothing in the way of promoting relationship knowledge and skill. Teachers get pay raises based on their capacity to increase students' academic multiple-choice test scores, not on their ability to teach students how to relate to each other. This emphasis on academic achievement at all cost continues in spite of the fact that truancy, school vandalism, bullying, dropouts, and student suicides are at all-time highs in schools, regardless of whether they are in located in small towns, suburbs, or large cities.

I'm not sure why we ignore the obvious fact that we, parents and teachers alike, are failing to "educate" our children in how to relate to others. I believe the reason for this lack arises, in part, from the assumption that the ability to relate to others is somehow inherited through our genes and that children will mysteriously "pick up" what they need to know about forming relationships as they grow from infancy into adulthood. If this assumption is correct, then something is very wrong with our genes and the mysterious process that is supposed to facilitate our development into fully functioning happy and satisfied adults.

> **"...truancy, school vandalism, bullying, dropouts, and student suicides are at all-time highs in schools..."**

I do not believe that making relationships work is a simple activity that we somehow inherit the knack of doing. Making friends and keeping them is one of the most difficult and crucial tasks we face as human beings. It takes time, effort, and most importantly, knowledge and skill to do well. Clearly, physical appearance and certain aspects of temperament may be inherited, but most of what goes into being successful at making friends is learned. This learning takes place first within the home through parents' modeling and teaching, and it is later applied and modified outside the home in interactions with playmates and school-aged peers in educational and social situations.

Parents, you need to be aware that children will learn the basics of relating from you. You do not have a choice of whether or not to teach your children about relationships; you only have a choice about how and what to teach them. I have found in my studies that relationships go through a constant process—a choice, a beginning, a deepening, and an ending. Continually changing communication skills are needed to progress successfully from one stage of a relationship to the next.

While most of us are aware of the usefulness of verbal skills in making known our needs and desires to others, the importance of nonverbal communication skills is often overlooked. Nonverbal errors—standing too close, staring for too long, adopting an angry facial expression when not really feeling angry—can be relationship killers. The foundation for future relationship forays is built during the first two years of a child's life when nonverbal ways of relating obviously predominate. To enable children to "connect" with others in meaningful ways, parents and other caregivers need to teach children how to express feelings and read them in others through facial expressions, tones of voice, gestures, postures, touch, and respect for personal space. Because nonverbal communications and relationships themselves become more subtle and complex over time, this teaching needs to begin in infancy and continue throughout childhood.

Parents are forever teachers. The teaching you do is much more effective if it takes place in a warm, nurturing environment in which children feel safe and protected. Let me give you an example of what I mean from my own childhood. I was raised in the inner city of Milwaukee by an Italian mother and a Polish father. For most of my childhood, my parents and I lived in a small apartment that was one of a number of flats and apartments making up a two-house complex owned by my mother's Italian parents. My various Italian aunts, uncles, and cousins lived within and around this complex. My extended Italian family, "the Padovanos," was a very large and very colorful one.

One winter day when I was about eight years old, I did something in school that I shouldn't have done. Mrs. Zinsminski, my third-grade teacher, decided that I must stay after school and write 500 times that I would not misbehave again. She called my mother to tell her that she was keeping me after school. My mother replied that she didn't want me to stay late at school because a storm was coming. She was concerned that I might get caught in the storm walking home. Mrs Zinsminski, however, was not to be dissuaded. I was at my desk writing the sentences after school when I heard a noise at the back of the room. I turned around and saw twenty-three

Padovanos! The word had gone out from one family member to another that I was in need of help and support. "Stevie" was being keep after school when a storm was coming.

Mrs. Zinsminski had taught for a long time in my neighborhood and realized that discretion was the better part of valor. She wisely decided that maybe the weather did look threatening and that I should go home. My family did not let me off the hook; I still had to complete the sentences at home. But I will always remember how safe, protected, and loved I felt as I walked home that dreary, gray Milwaukee day, literally surrounded by my family. This is what I wish for all children to feel within their own families.

My simple plea, request, wish, demand, directive, suggestion, desire, and hope is that you do not abdicate your own responsibility for teaching your children about relationships and that you act as responsible change agents in your schools to help educators see the importance of teaching relationship skills. In that way many other children, like Amy who you met earlier, will learn not only how to add and subtract, but also how to build relationships that may last a lifetime.

Stephen Nowicki Jr. *received his B.A. from Carroll College, his M.S. from Marquette University and his Ph.D. from Purdue University. He completed his clinical psychology internship at Duke University Medical Center. He is the author of over 225 publications and presentations and the coauthor of four books. During his thirty years of teaching at Emory University, he has served as Director of Clinical Training and head of the Emory University Counseling Center. Steve was a corecipient of the Applied Reseacher of the Year award in 1997 given by the AAAP division of the American Psychological Society. He received an Emory Williams Teaching Award and is the Charles Howard Candler Professor of Psychology. A Diplomate in Applied Psychology, he continues to be a consultant to public and private schools and maintains an active clinical practice. In his spare time, he is an avid golfer, hiker, and tennis player. He and his wife, Kaaren, have one son.*

Jane Stoodt Attanucci

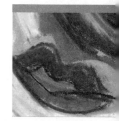

Parenting Adolescents

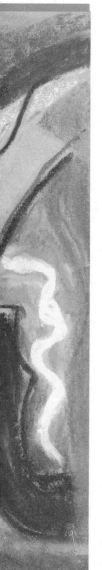

𝓜*y second and last child* left for college *last fall.* I am no longer an everyday parent of adolescents, but I come to the task of writing this essay with considerable experience. In addition to my own years of adolescence in the sixties, I spent six years raising two middle schoolers in the eighties and eight consecutive years as a parent of high school students in the nineties. And that doesn't include my decades of research and teaching college students in a course called Adolescent Development.

Yet with all of my experience and knowledge, I approach writing about parenting adolescents with great humility. I know what I know; but I know, too, what I don't know.

I know that culture shapes adolescence and that my experience is primarily Euro-American. I know that some young people struggle deeply in body, mind, and soul during adolescence and that neither my own children nor I experienced the classic storm and stress that plague so many others. I know that, unlike talking or writing about raising younger children, talking and writing about parenting adolescents includes the adolescents as active listeners and as potential readers and critics. Their demands for respect are justified, and their expectations for complex, not simplistic, representations are valid.

Understanding the teen years is an awesome challenge. Too often I have heard colleagues talk about the parallels between adolescence and the "terrible twos," a tantrum-filled stage when toddlers struggle for autonomy. Not fair and not true. As we try to gain insight into these difficult years, perhaps it would be more fruitful to look at one of the stages in author and psychoanalyst Erik H. Erikson's life cycle of developmental crises—that dilemma shared by parents and adolescents alike, the conflict between trust and doubt.

Recalling my children's adolescent years—especially those times when they wanted to go somewhere I didn't want them to go—I can still hear myself saying to them: "It's not that I don't trust you. It's just that I don't trust the others, and I'm wary of the situation." (I assume some readers have said or heard this line before.) I really believed myself at the time. I didn't hear my words as rationalizations. I didn't recognize my own fears and doubts. I can now see that I was fearful of letting my kids move into unfamiliar circumstances without me. I failed to realize that the unfamiliarity was sometimes my own, not always theirs. Adolescents often know things adults do not know, even granting adults years more experience. Moreover, adolescents can and do learn outside the protective walls of parental love and surveillance.

If I had felt the complete trust that I claimed to feel, then I would have had confidence in my adolescent children's abilities to make judgments for themselves, to negotiate solutions with their friends, and to create situations that were both safe and fun. In many cases, I was able to do just that. Other times, I needed to realize that I had doubts and to find reasonable ways to express those doubts to my children. There were also occasions when I needed to listen to my adolescents' doubts about my judgments. The growing up involved us all.

Trust between parents and adolescents has multiple layers and nuances. Even though on one level I sincerely trusted my children, on another level I was letting my doubts overshadow that trust. In my standard line about mistrusting others, I was failing to express faith in my kids' judgment, in their ability to handle difficult situations. I was also failing to tell the truth about my inner fears. My children knew it. I don't think I understood my own fears and ambivalence until they had subsided considerably and I was able to see my children as the young adults they had become. I remember laughing at myself with my college students when my "line" appeared in a case study we were reading for class. The ironies were not lost on them.

> **Adolescents often know things adults do not know, even granting adults years more experience.**

Especially when their children reach adolescence, parents are often adamant that their teens tell the truth. They want them to be honest and forthcoming about their whereabouts, associations, and affections. These same parents, though, may retreat into an angry defensiveness when their honest and forthright young sons or daughters pry too aggressively into their personal lives or pasts, or point out their hypocrisies. Once again, it is a matter of balance between trust and doubt. There are times when parents and children need to express their doubts, to demand total honesty and openness. And there are times when parents and children must trust each other. A family builds the most satisfying dialogues on a mutual respect that includes tolerance for differences, appreciation for good judgments, recognition of privacy needs, and forgiveness for failures and frailties.

So, what is my best advice? Take seriously both trusting and doubting each other in a respectful and loving way. Realize that things that remain unspoken can be as important to identity and relationships as those things openly declared. Avoid thinking of trust as an all or nothing proposition. Accept the fact that there will always be doubts and then find a balance between the trust and the doubts.

151

The years when your children are adolescents can be one of the most rewarding times for you as a parent. Don't back off now. Stay involved in your teens' lives. Take an active part, one that goes beyond parent-teacher conferences, in the school community. Volunteer for a community service project and tag along with your kids and their friends. Pay attention to other people's children and join an activity that is not directly related to your own child. Renew old interests and discover new ones as your children are doing the same. Make friends. Adolescents understand deeply the value of friendship. With any luck, someday your adult children will tell you how much they appreciated your parental care, and they will be among your best friends.

152

Jane Stoodt Attanucci *was born in Chicago and currently lives in Lexington, Massachusetts, where she is Associate Professor of Psychology and Human Development at Wheelock College. Jane received her B.A. from Emmanuel College in 1973 and her Ed.D. at Harvard in 1984. She has worked with children for more than twenty-five years as either a researcher or teacher. Jane is the author or coauthor of more than fifteen scholarly articles dealing with child development. She was a postdoctoral Fellow of the National Academy of Education in 1990. She is the mother of two children and with her husband, John, enjoys walking, movies, and folk concerts.*

Disobedience is the infant's first

step towards autonomy.

—LEWIS MUMFORD

Michael K. Levine

Advice
for Your
Young Adults

$\mathcal{I}$*have been a practicing pediatrician since 1963, and I have seen a great many changes* in our patterns of living over nearly four decades. Observing these changes prompted me to develop a list of suggestions for parents whose children are getting ready to leave home to enter the job market, college, or military service. It is my hope that this list will aid parents in advising their young adults so they can enter this challenging world with confidence, assurance, and self-respect.

Treat all people with respect from the moment you meet them. First impressions can be misleading. Just because someone is poor or unwashed does not mean that he or she is uneducated or stupid.

Remember that every person you meet is unique. Show an interest in people, ask them questions, and listen to what they have to say. You will learn a great deal this way. When you meet people from different backgrounds (in other words, most of the people you will encounter), make an effort to learn something of their culture—and, if possible, some of their language. If you can transmit your interest in their culture, other people will know that you care about them as individuals.

Cultivate the art of patience. You will need it every day. Some people don't communicate as well as others and really do need more of your time and attention. Learn to recognize who they are, to appreciate their needs and demands on your time, and to listen patiently to their suggestions or complaints. This technique will help you do your job better and will help you gain other people's respect. People remember when someone takes the time for them.

You will occasionally run into people you cannot relate to, no matter how patient you are and no matter how much time you give them. Be willing to recognize this, and learn diplomatic ways to work around those people.

If you go to college, remember your school after graduation and donate money as often as you can. That is the institution that gave you the opportunity to do what you really wanted to do in life.

No matter what career you choose, you must realize that you cannot learn it all. There is too much. Accept that fact, and stay as current in your field of interest as you can without compromising your family life. Ask for expert help when you need it, and make it a point to keep learning from your colleagues.

After you leave home, don't forget your parents and grandparents as a source of advice and wisdom. When you don't know what to do and are a long way from home, think of them. Your family is the best resource you have. They not only have a lot of experience but also care about you and have your interests at heart.

Keep smiling, and never lose your sense of humor. You have to be a little crazy now and then in order to get along with and work with a wide variety of people. If you can defuse a tense situation with humor, it will be healthy for everyone.

Michael K. Levine, *a native of Massachusetts, received his B.A. and M.D. degrees from Tufts University. He has been a practicing pediatrician since 1963, has served on the faculty of the Emory University School of Medicine, and among other positions has served as president of the medical staff at Scottish Rite Children's Medical Center in Atlanta. Michael is especially interested in children with attention deficit disorders and learning disabilities. He has contributed regularly to the medical and popular literature and is a regular guest on radio and television shows concerning children and their health. He has received the Physician's Recognition award from the American Medical Association. Outside of work, he has served as docent at the High Museum of Art in Atlanta and enjoys jogging, reading, and travel. Michael and his wife, Esther, have two grown children.*

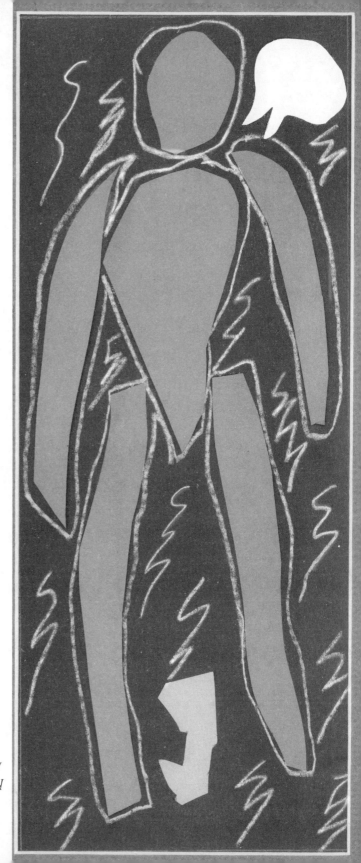

No matter how calmly you try to referee, parenting will eventually produce bizarre behavior, and I'm not talking about the kids. *Their* behavior is always normal.

—BILL COSBY
Fatherhood

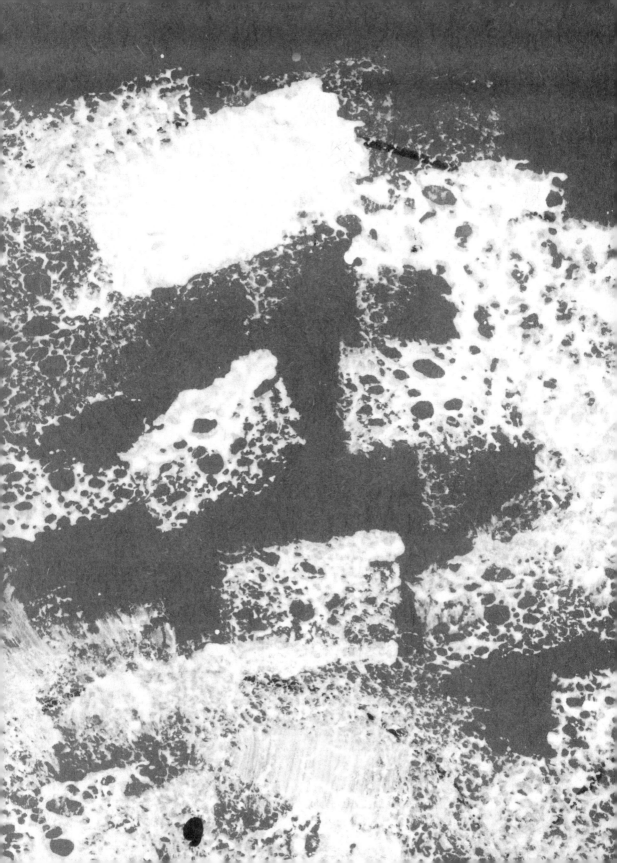

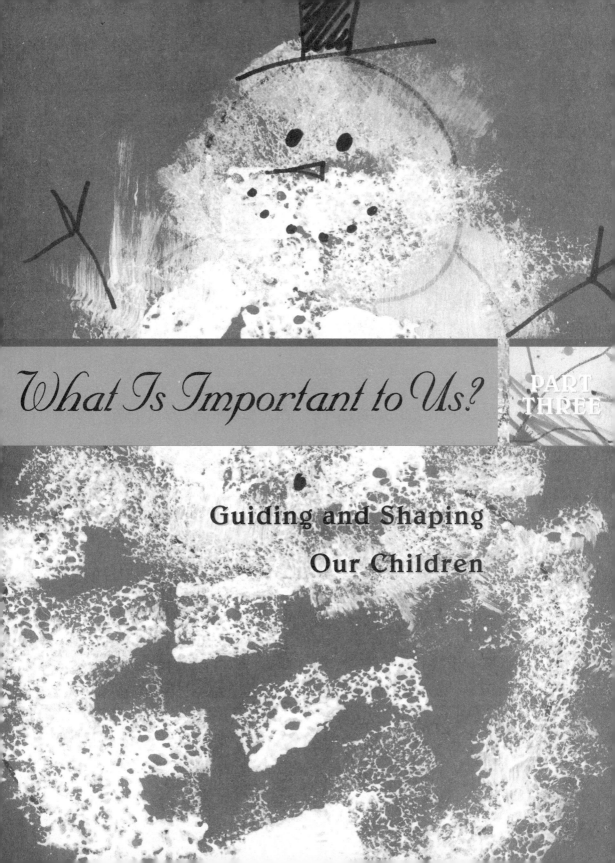

What Is Important to Us?

PART THREE

Guiding and Shaping

Our Children

"*How to*" *books for parents* have been around for literally thousands of years (guidelines for child rearing date back to the first century AD), and yet we still approach the enterprise of parenting with the same confusion and apprehension with which our own parents faced the task of raising us. Two things are certain: 1) Our parents were imperfect people who tried their best with us and fell short in some places and excelled in others; and 2) No matter how hard we try, our children will someday realize that we too are imperfect.

So what are we to do?

The essays in this section offer specific ideas, sometimes in the form of direct wisdom-driven lists, other times as do's and don'ts embedded in a narrative context. Some suggestions are born of success: "These things worked for me. Try them!" Others were born of failure: "This didn't work for me. Don't try it!" Wisdom about raising children arises from a combination of success and failure wrapped up in a love-based commitment to do the right thing more often than we do the wrong—and a determination not to repeat the wrong if we can possibly help it!

Diane P. Monnier

"Are You the Library Girl?"

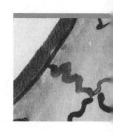

Are you the Library Girl?" I heard the small voice behind me ask. "I sure am," was my quick response as I turned to see a little girl about four years old standing before me. Her mother, directly behind her, smiled and said, "That's the librarian, honey."

While something inside of me really liked "The Library Girl" label, it doesn't really convey the entire picture. It is the long series of connections between that young child, her parent, the library, the books, and the librarian that allows me to get up each morning ready for the questions and answers that are the joys of my profession.

The public library—whether it's a large metropolitan building with myriad computers and books galore or a bookmobile that stops at a shopping center twice a month—remains the single American institution where children and their parents can explore together the magic of the written word.

What about bookstores or toy stores with wonderful areas of children's books, you ask? True, in the new millennium parents and children can exercise more options when it comes to obtaining books. However, the public library still remains the one place where we can hold the books in our hands and explore their wonder at our leisure. And, perhaps best of all, on each visit to the library a child may take some of that wonder home for free to savor over and over.

Librarians are partners with parents in the important job of raising lifelong readers. I urge parents to let that partnership begin when the child is very young. Many parents ask how old a child must be before they start visiting the public library. There is no magical Library Fairy who swoops down and taps a child on the head declaring, "Now, this one is ready to explore the library." With today's variety of books for children—board books for infants, lift-the-flap books for toddlers, and a huge array of picture books and chapter books for older children—the library is the perfect place to visit with children of any age.

A few years ago, with the help of a wonderful start-up grant, Bethesda Regional Library launched a program for infants and their parents. We received permission from the American Library Association to use the BORN TO READ name for our programs, which feature books (yes, we read books to babies), music, nursery rhymes, and simple language development activities for babies from birth to eighteen months of age.

We learned a lot that first year, mostly from the babies themselves. We provided programs for six-month-olds who smiled a lot while sitting on Mommy's lap and for twelve-month-olds who never stopped moving during the entire half-hour. We came to understand how various ages require different types of activities. But, perhaps more important, we realized how differently individual children behave. Some one-year-olds will sit and listen to a story for an extended period of time, while others are constantly moving and exploring. What we continue to share with parents is the notion that children who are moving, playing with a ball, seemingly not paying attention, are still receiving language.

After two years of offering BORN TO READ, we reconsidered the age range and decided to invite twelve- to twenty-four-month-olds to attend a different program, one that offered more physical activity geared for this busy age. We call these sessions GROW TO READ and continue to read books and foster early language development skills while encouraging these older babies to jump like a frog, hop like a bunny, and reach up high for a twinkling star. We still remember that some children would rather sit quietly and watch. That's okay, too.

Our goals? To model book-related activities to parents and caregivers, encouraging them to read to their children right from the beginning of their lives. One of my treasured possessions is a picture of me reading GOODNIGHT

> ❝ *No computer, no new millennium technology will replace the importance of reading in the life of a child.* ❞

MOON by Margaret Wise Brown to my grandson on the very first day of his life. True, his eyes were closed, but I know he heard my voice, and that is the important part. Parents who talk, read, and sing to their children are giving gifts that reap future dividends again and again.

Almost twenty years ago, Jim Trelease wrote THE READ ALOUD HANDBOOK. He is well-known now as a public speaker as well as an author, and he continues to promote the read-aloud message—read to your children, and keep reading aloud even when your children learn to read on their own.

Librarians have said that to parents for years, and we are delighted that many of them make reading-aloud part of their family ritual. Remember the books you loved as a child? How much fun you'll have sharing a favorite like BLUEBERRIES FOR SAL by Robert McCloskey or MY FATHER'S DRAGON by Ruth Stiles Gannett with your own children.

163

Every summer librarians link families with books about the people and places they might encounter on their vacations—AND, THEN, WHAT HAPPENED, PAUL REVERE? by Jean Fritz for the family exploring Boston together, or Rhoda Blumberg's THE GREAT AMERICAN GOLD RUSH for another group going to California. How exciting for a family traveling to Canada to share ANNE OF GREEN GABLES by Lucy Maud Montgomery as a pre-trip read-aloud. Even if a family plans a stay-at-home summer, the public library's multitude of resources will take them on fantastic journeys to places real and imaginary.

Don't be reluctant to march right up to your local librarian and ask for suggestions of books for your child to read alone or for you to share as a family. Putting just the right book into the hands of a child is what librarians love best, and, oh, how wonderful it is when that child returns the next week asking for "another one just as good."

Of course, no librarian can guarantee that children who come from homes where reading is emphasized will get straight A's or wind up with perfect SAT scores, but we do know that children who can't read will struggle in school and throughout their entire lives. No computer, no new millennium technology will replace the importance of reading in the life of a child.

To cultivate and nurture lifelong readers, start early and introduce your child to books that inform and delight, books of fiction and wonderful nonfiction. Exploring all the treasures waiting in a public library is a never-ending adventure. Don't wait another day to begin your child's journey.

Diane P. Monnier *began her work with children in 1965 as a high school English teacher. She subsequently worked with preschoolers, teaching three- and four-year-olds in Florida and Texas. After receiving her library degree from the University of Oklahoma, Diane expanded her career to become a children's librarian. She is currently Regional Children's Librarian at the Bethesda Regional Library in Maryland. Diane is a member of the selection committee for the Best Books for Young Adults award, given by the American Library Association. She and her husband live in Gaithersburg, Maryland.*

Barbara Ellison Rosenblit

A Tango, a Two-Step

It's not completely clear that teachers have *much valuable advice to offer parents.* I am a teacher and a parent, and I am accustomed over these many years to giving advice to parents, mostly because they seem to want it so badly. They envy our behavioral formulas and charts and covet the heralded notions of consistency, clarity, and limit-setting that are the teacher's stock-in-trade. But here's the rub: teachers don't really love your child the way you do.

Oh, they may appreciate his clever mind or be grateful that she is so neat and polite. But they neither know nor appreciate the deeply unusual gene bank that gave birth, all these many generations later, to this product of chance, that set of chromosomes assembled from all those generations of nonconformists and freethinkers of which the family is so proud. Teachers don't see Uncle Frank's faraway stare that defined his dreamy mind when they look at your boy; they see instead a child "off-task." They don't appreciate Aunt Sooky's electrically charged but skewed view of the world that was thankfully reborn in your girl; they see instead an iconoclast. When parents look at a child, they should see the product of centuries of genetic non-manipulation. Teachers see that too, but they're not as happy about it.

But I am here to tell you what I, the teacher, have learned of parenting. First of all, teaching is easier. I know much more about the vagaries of teaching, that precious work that can inspire or damage, that can frame a life of value or of disappointment. What does my experience in the classroom have to teach about raising children? Raising children has taught me more about teaching than the other way around.

Keep in mind that the learning curve in both teaching and parenting isn't up and up. If it were, we teachers wouldn't still be trying to decide how to teach reading or what in the devil to do with the new technology, how to respectfully eulogize grammar, or how to retrieve the precious quiet that used to precede thought. And we parents wouldn't be asking, as if for the first time, at what age to toilet train or whether children grow out of toeing-in when they walk, or whether organized sports before age six is a good idea. We should have known the answers to all that eons ago, and we could have moved on to planting microchips in our brains and not crying over confusion about what we don't understand.

But here is what I do know. Teaching and parenting share a basic and important feature: Neither happens as a solo act; each needs a partner. There are always at least two involved in the enterprise, never monologues but rather dialogues—even if the other guy sometimes seems to be silent. Consequently, the relationship of teacher to student, like that of parent to child, is risky—not a set of prechoreographed and not-too-dangerous moves, or actions, or rubrics. It is a glorious dance with a partner, full of swirls and dips and chancy spins, one in which sometimes one partner leads, sometimes the other. It is exhausting. The music is sometimes a tango and sometimes a two-step and once in a while, for a few incredible reckless moments, a jitterbug with athletic leaps. If you don't see the poetry and the music in this work, in teaching, in parenting, it will never be your calling.

I offer three teaching notions to keep in mind while raising a child. I take them from years of teaching and they seem to apply to parenting quite fairly. Remember the cardinal difference in application: Love is a commodity found in the home, not the classroom. Teachers can fill the love gap with humor or amusement, charts or action plans, but unconditional love and acceptance are in the parents' domain exclusively. That critical difference makes parenting much easier, and much harder.

Do no harm. Keep this credo in the sight lines of your every action. A psychologist once let our faculty in on one of his dirty little secrets. He said that when he engages in therapy sessions with a client, it is almost guaranteed that some moment of humiliation or hurt from the client's school days makes its way to the surface, digging out from twenty or thirty years of other deposits, long buried, but far from dead. The client may be twenty—or fifty—or eighty—it doesn't matter; school stuff is there for the excavation. Parents have it even harder. We make plenty of mistakes—some witting, some unwitting—that our children will remember ruefully. We can love our children and treat them with respect, and have hope, but it's hard to lose the notion that we are providing grist for the therapeutic mill. We know full well when a word, a look, an angrily uttered half-truth is meant to hurt, designed to wound. That's when we have to stop ourselves. Do no harm.

> **"*Love is a commodity found in the home, not the classroom.* "**

Be humble. When you think you have just taught your child the best lesson in the history of humankind, chances are good you didn't. Do you know Akira Kurosawa's classic film on point of view, *Rashomon*? The film uses the point of view premise to replay a rape from multiple perspectives: the rapist's, the woman raped, her husband's, and a stranger watching from the bushes. This is a movie about point of view, but it is also about the set of assumptions that outline and color our perceptions, changing the motives and abilities of the key players, based not on any measured truth, but on which set of eyes is doing the looking. One event, four scripts. Move this technique to the classroom and exaggerate for amusement's sake. We'll visit the same event through the eyes of the teacher, the supervisor, and the student. You'll get the point.

The teacher is up front teaching her heart out. It's one of those unmistakable lessons attentive to multiple intelligences and learning styles and brain-based learning, supported by visual grids and charts and small-group activities, armed with half a dozen rubrics to measure learning and alternative assessment techniques for those who have learning or attention deficits. Every workshop she's attended for the last three years has its ghost somewhere in today's lesson. And, from her glance around to gauge interest, the students do all seem to be following her as she moves about from map to grid to chart to group.

> **"Keep in mind that the learning curve in both teaching and parenting isn't up and up."**

Enter the supervisor. With her sharp professional eye, she recognizes a well-ordered classroom, notes the orderly arrangement of student desks which allows visibility for everyone (hmm . . . there are three desks not being used; must alert maintenance), is gratified to see that the nature posters with inspirational messages are all laminated according to school policy and that the bulletin board itself is relevant to the subject (this is history class, isn't it?). The supervisor makes a mental note to remember to commend Ms. Teacher for her recent willingness to take an unscheduled lunch duty when asked.

Now, let's saw into the cranial lobe of the students and see what they see. Yeah, there's a teacher up front. Remember the blurry, pulsating dot over the faces of guests on talk shows who don't want to be recognized? Well, sure enough, there it is, over the teacher's face. Slightly overweight and (here's the weird part) emitting sounds reminiscent of, well, white noise, she's bobbing around the room—getting close, moving back. The student knows enough to follow the glowing ball as it moves. To stay out of trouble, every student knows to keep an eye on the ball.

Okay, maybe I went too far with this one, but I'm closer than any of us probably cares to believe.

Transfer the movie set to your house. Only this time you stand armed with your array of parenting classes and books and a set of forbidden phrases from your own parents that you have sworn will never cross your lips, and there is this child to be disciplined looking at you. Only not really looking. Well, not seeing in any case. He too sees the pulsating dot over your face and hears the white noise that comes out of your mouth, which he will later describe as "screaming."

In child-talk, "screaming" means "speaking directly to me and not to someone else in the room," as in "You just stood there screaming at me!" You reply softly, "But I wasn't screaming," and he stares at you like you've lost your mind and repeats that you were screaming. If this scene were under the scrutiny of a grandparent, he might commend you, thinking you perhaps a bit unemotional, but on the right track. But if a sibling were there, your "screaming" would be unequivocally confirmed.

So what's the point? Well, don't assume that your perspective is the only one. You can even try to look at the situation through the child's eyes. But don't let your attempt at understanding paralyze you. After all, you see some things that nobody else can see. And you can see further.

Act as if you care. In the classroom, play like you care about every student and, miraculously, eventually you will. At home, act as though you care about your child even if you don't feel like you do at the moment. There's a lot of research out there on self-esteem. *This isn't about that.* This one is about those assumptions we make about other people that influence us and affect our ability to value what they do.

Back in 1968, two researchers, Robert Rosenthal and Lenore Jacobson, published their famous, albeit controversial, report called Pygmalion in the Classroom about the effect of teacher expectation on student achievement. They claimed to have measured a certain "expectancy bias" that teachers develop when they hold given (and, in this experiment, untrue) beliefs about student ability, and they claimed to show that preferred treatment alone can affect student performance. After the publication of their work, the research was harshly criticized on methodological grounds, and the outcomes were never replicated by later researchers.

But anyone who has ever been introspective about teaching, anyone who understands the power to damage inherent in a look or gesture or touch, anyone who is honest enough to recognize the set of assumptions and prejudices that afflict us as we gaze across that sea of eyes and ears and funny-colored hair will admit, however quietly, that the theory exposes a crucial area of student achievement, one within our control, not theirs. And being a parent holds tenfold the destructive power in a look of disappointment, lips pursed in disapproval. The trick is to provide an environment that reinforces that you care, even if you are disappointed or angry.

More research on the classroom followed by Jere E. Brophy and Thomas E. Good. They went into classrooms, had teachers identify their "best" students, and spent hours watching how teachers interacted with them and with other "less able" students, trying to measure what they called "differential treatment." They noticed that students who were perceived as "able" were given more chances to answer questions, were given longer to think about answers, and when they had difficulty, the teacher would delve, give clues, or rephrase more willingly than with "low achievers." The research showed a warmer socio-emotional atmosphere—teachers would smile more, nod more, and lean toward "brighter" students, looking more directly into their eyes, in general being "friendlier" toward them. You get the idea.

Does this research transfer to the home? It is not about liking every student, and it is not about liking your child every minute of the day. You can't and you won't. But you can act as if you do.

Watch how you treat your child when he pleases you, and then when your child irritates you because of a slouch or sneer or pierced whatever. Imagine one of those other moments, the cherished ones, instead. Smile at him, joke a little, treat her like you would if she were the daughter you wished she were. Stretch to make your child matter, even at those difficult moments. It works. It works in the classroom, and it works at home. You change. He changes. Both for the better.

Three notions—doing no harm, having some humility, and showing the children that you like them—are a good beginning. Now love your child, then listen for the music that will set it all in motion, and go enjoy the dance.

Barbara Ellison Rosenblit *received a B.A. in English and American literature from Brandeis University, an M.A. in English from Columbia University Teachers College, and an M.A. in Jewish studies from Emory University. For many years Barbara taught English in a Peace Corps-like program in the Negev Desert, and in the United States she has served as a curriculum coordinator and as director of a middle school. In 1997, as one of the top 100 teachers of excellence, she was a delegate to the U. S. Department of Education Teacher Forum. Barbara and her husband have three children.*

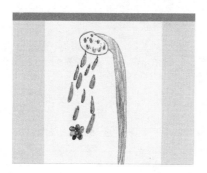

A wise parent humours the desire
for independent action, so as to
become the friend and advisor
when his absolute rule shall cease.

—Elizabeth Gaskell

Ron Luckie

You Are Your Child's First Teacher

During more than forty years of working *with children in schools,* I have watched and listened to and talked with a great many children and parents and teachers. Through those observations and conversations, I have discovered certain principles about children and teaching that I think will be helpful for any parent. After all, as a parent you are your child's first teacher.

Children need to be encouraged more than they need correction. Encouragement is not needed occasionally. It is needed often, constantly, and it must be offered with purpose.

I have known this truth for many years, but it came home to me most clearly when I helped my granddaughter learn to walk. She was standing across the room holding onto a chair. I said, "Callie, come over here to Gramps and give me a hug." She looked at me, smiled, and let go of the chair. I said, "Great! Now walk over here." She made two teetering steps and fell on her bottom. She sat there looking at me. I said, "Great try. Let's do it again. You can do it. That was a great try." She crawled to the chair, pulled up, and got her balance. I motioned for her to come to me. She made two or three more steps, and this time fell face forward. She looked a little frightened. I simply said, "That was a much better try," and continued to hold my hands out to her. Finally, after many attempts, she walked all the way across the room into my arms, and we hugged, danced around the room, and celebrated. It was a wonderful experience for a grandfather.

> ❝ *Confident people find a way to be competent.* ❞

176

With some reflection on the incident, it occurred to me that not one time did I tell my granddaughter she had failed. The truth is, she was unsuccessful many more times than she was successful. It further occurred to me that if we taught our children how to walk in the same way we teach them reading and math skills, they would probably still be moving about on all fours.

Raising children and teaching them is more about encouragement than it is about correction. Children need vast amounts of encouragement with only some correction.

Helping your child acquire confidence is more important than teaching your child competence. The world is full of competent people who are able to accomplish little because they lack confidence. Confident people find a way to be competent. Build your children's confidence by praising and encouraging them. Show your children that you value their ideas, opinions, and suggestions.

Teaching your child is more about motivation than it is about instruction. In order to teach children something, first help them see the challenge and the possibility to meet it, and then get out of the way. During your years of childrearing, you will need a vast repertoire of methods—a myriad of approaches to motivation. Here are a few pointers from experienced, effective teachers to keep in mind as you motivate your child to learn.

Expect much, get much.

Look for ways to make learning easy, not difficult. Children need to perceive a task as possible.

Keep the task challenging. There is a fine balance between making learning easy and making it uninteresting.

Set reasonable goals and explain them clearly. Children are more likely to be motivated when they understand the purpose of their effort.

Help your child overcome the fear of failure. Most people do not succeed immediately at a new task. Lack of success is not failure. Failure is no longer trying.

Find ways to show your children that they are making progress, and praise even small successes.

Share with your children and allow them to share with you.

Celebrate achievements, even small achievements, on a daily basis.

Reward effort. Show your approval!

Children need to know how to learn. The expansion of knowledge has made it impossible for a person to know everything about anything, much less to know everything about everything. What should we expect our schools to teach our children? We must see that they teach skills and attitudes toward learning that will support our children for a lifetime, long after they have left the classroom. As parents, we should keep a close eye on our children's schools and demand that they train our children in *how to learn* by teaching the following skills: communication (reading, writing, listening, speaking); computation; intellectual proficiencies (gathering, analyzing, and summarizing information and making decisions), and healthy attitudes (confidence, a positive approach to life, and an appreciation of work, fun, and beauty).

This assignment may sound serious and difficult and somewhat overwhelming. But teaching a child, whether as a parent or as a professional, brings many rewards along with all the challenges.

As you raise your children, have fun. Don't take yourself too seriously. Be willing to admit sometimes that you are wrong. And above all, listen to and see the beauty in each child.

Ron Luckie *was born in Alabama in 1933. He received a B.A. from Samford University in 1955 and an M.Ed. and Ph.D. in education from the University of Southern Mississippi in 1963. As a teacher and principal for more than forty-four years, Ron's focus has been on children's study skills. He is coauthor of STUDY POWER, a book published in 1998. Ron and his wife, Mary, have two grown children. He also pursues the hobbies of fishing, reading, and music.*

Children have more need of models than of critics.

—JOSEPH JOUBERT
Pensées

Pearlie Craft Dove

Educating Our Children

As we enter the next millennium, most of us are aware of society's ever-increasing need for *superior teachers.* We all hope that the profession will attract the best minds, the ablest citizens, and the strongest believers in the democratic ideal. We expect our children's teachers to enjoy their work for the satisfaction it provides and to be proud of the service they render. We hope that they believe "all children are educable" and that they will have the persistence to pursue that challenge. We pray that these people into whose hands we deliver our children will instill in them a lifelong love of learning.

We cannot, however, leave the entire burden of educating our children on our teachers' shoulders. Long before we turn our children over to the educational system, we should begin to lay the groundwork that will prepare them to take full advantage of the learning process. In my thirty-nine years as an educator, I have come to realize that the very qualities that make the best teachers are the same ones that make the best learners. My advice—from one parent to another—and my plea—from a teacher to all parents—is for you to instill in your children from an early age these four things: persistence, a love for learning, a respect for other human beings and tolerance of differences, and a simple yet sound social philosophy. How much easier and more rewarding our teachers' jobs would be if students came to them already possessing these qualities.

Encourage your children to persevere as they grow and learn. With persistence, almost everyone can achieve some degree of success in some areas of learning. Help your children to see that although they will always encounter obstacles and difficult challenges, if they develop the patience to persist, they can accomplish more than they ever thought possible.

Calvin Coolidge expressed his belief in the power of persistence in these words:

> *Nothing in this world can take the place of persistence. Talent will not; nothing is more common than unsuccessful people with talent. Genius will not; unrewarded genius is almost a proverb. Education will not; the world is full of educated derelicts. Persistence and determination alone are omnipotent. The slogan "press on" has solved and always will solve the problems of the human race.*

Give your children an appetite for learning. This gift will stay with them throughout their lives. You can help your children acquire a love for discovery well before they begin formal schooling. Encourage your children to observe and describe the people and things around them. Give them opportunities to converse with older people. Listen to song lyrics and musical scores with them. Read the Bible and view the beauty of nature with them. Expose them to artists' masterpieces and memorize poetic verses with them. No one can become fully educated in school, no matter

how long or how good the schooling. Our concern as parents must be with making our children receptive to learning.

> **❝ You can teach even the youngest children something about getting along with other people. ❞**

Teach your children to respect all human beings despite their differences. History has taught us that we have become a strong nation because of our diversity. Help children to see that we're all important parts of this great American mosaic made up of many peoples—from the original inhabitants of our land, to the first arrivals on the Mayflower, to the latest immigrants. And we must build in our children a feeling of global connectedness. With advances in communication and technology, children are aware of things outside their own community at a younger and younger age. Teach them how to accept, respect, and appreciate all human beings without regard to religious beliefs, ethnic origins, customs, or economic conditions.

Teach your children that they can make the world a better place. Although it may seem to be expecting too much to advise you to instill in your children a sound social philosophy, such a goal is not at all unrealistic. You can teach even the youngest children something about getting along with other people. From the time children can talk, they can begin to learn that they can do something to improve conditions in society. At a very young age, they can understand that there are times when the needs of the larger group have to come before the rights of the individual or of a certain special-interest group. As a parent you not only can transmit traditional values to your children, you also can show them ways to promote the social good.

Your children's teachers will thank you, your children's future employers and colleagues will thank you, and someday your children will thank you if you give them these lasting gifts: the ability to persist in worthwhile pursuits in spite of obstacles

183

and challenges, a love of learning, a respect for other human beings, and a sound social philosophy.

These qualities, the very ones we demand in our children's teachers, are the ones we should strive to develop as we raise our children. Indeed, they are desirable for all who share the American Dream.

Pearlie Craft Dove *received a B.A. from Clark College, an M.A. from Atlanta University, and an Ed.D. from the University of Colorado at Boulder. She has worked directly and indirectly with children for over thirty-nine years. Pearlie is professor emerita at Clark Atlanta University, where she had been Distinguished Professor of Education and chair of the Department of Education. Among other positions, she has served on the National Executive Committee for the Association of Teacher Educators, on the Board of Directors for the American Association of Colleges for Teacher Education, and as a Rosalynn Carter Fellow at Emory Institute for Women's Studies. Pearlie is active in community events, historic preservation, and the arts. She and her husband, Jackson, had two daughters, one of whom is a teacher.*

The greatest gifts my parents gave to me... were
their unconditional love and a set of values.
Values that they lived and didn't just lecture
about. Values that included an understanding of
the simple difference between right and wrong,
a belief in God, the importance of hard work and
education, self-respect and a belief in America.

—COLIN POWELL
Parade Magazine

Mimi Brodsky Chenfeld

"...once I had brains," he said,
"and a heart also; so, having tried
them both, I should much rather
have a heart."

—L. FRANK BAUM
The Wizard of Oz

Listen with Your Heart

The Scarecrow wanted a brain. The Lion
wanted courage. The Tin Woodman wanted something else.

It has taken a lot of courage and a few brains to get through almost
fifty years of raising and working and playing with children of all
ages—from infancy to adulthood—but I am now convinced that it
was heart that kept me going. And I'm still at it. My heart is still in it.

I recently spent a day writing poetry with fifth graders, sharing
wonder with them, helping them put their ideas together. At the end
of the day their teacher confided to me that she had just been moved
up to fifth grade after years of teaching first graders.

"What a difference!" she exclaimed.

But, as we talked, we realized there were far more similarities than differences.

Later that night, I met with a group of high school teachers. The conversation turned to the special (often desperate) needs of our teens—some of them isolated and neglected, others hard-to-reach and incommunicative. One teacher said she suspected that middle and high school students stay up all night thinking of ways not to show you they're excited about something. Once again, we concluded with the insight that all of our children share certain needs.

Our task as parents or teachers is to recognize and respond to those needs.

After a day's residency as an Artist-in-the-School, I was packing up my "stuff" in the gym when a group of fourth and fifth graders came in with their teacher to rehearse a physical fitness demonstration. Even though I was all set to leave, I stayed to watch them in action. When they finished, I started for the door, waving good-bye.

> **"***Don't miss opportunities to just "be there" with your children.***"**

"Mimi! Thanks for watching us!" they called.

Don't miss opportunities to just "be there" with your children—watching them do their thing, becoming aware of their needs, listening to them. It's not so hard.

And when you are constantly around children, you must learn to listen with your heart. All of our children—no matter their ages or stages of development, no matter their backgrounds or personalities, no matter how communicative or incommunicative they may be—are speaking to us. I believe they are all saying something like this.

Pay attention to us. Listen to us. Be with us as we crawl, walk, run, talk, dance, sing, laugh, and cry along our journey.

Talk to us. Share your feelings and ideas with us. Be open to our thoughts and experiences. Know and understand who we are and what our daily lives are about.

Encourage us. Trust us. Celebrate our successes. Help us be strong and persistent through our many moments of failure.

Be patient. Be open. We have our own way of learning and developing. We're not robots. We are all unique individuals. Celebrate our originality.

Inspire us. Walk around with us, stopping to notice, listen, smell, and explore.

Remember that sometimes the simplest things are the best! The ride together to the dance class or the Little League game or the school play. Those precious few minutes hanging out together before bedtime or meals. Family songs and stories. Old games. Silly jokes. Just plain ordinary wonderful unprogrammed sharing of delight.

Don't overreact. Keep your cool. We all stumble, trip, and goof up as we grow.

Be firm, but do it with love. Make sure we know that your rules are demonstrations of your caring for us.

Be sure your actions and words match. We are watching you all the time. We notice everything you do—how you relate to others, what you care about, and what you're interested in. We know if you're respectful of others regardless of differences in backgrounds. We know if you're compassionate. We can tell if you care about our environment, our world.

Don't ask us to be good readers if you never read. Don't ask us to be good citizens, good neighbors if you don't reach out, don't respond to the hardships of others. We learn from you every day. We sniff hypocrisy.

Be honest and fair. We pick up on inconsistency. We learn to distrust phoniness.

Don't stop talking to us when we get older. We are listening to you even when you don't think we are. We understand a lot.

Keep your promises. We desperately want to trust you.

Make us feel safe and secure.

Tell us often that you cherish us.

So, on the "yellow brick road" of parenting, even when our courage fails us and our brains are exhausted, we can still offer our children our consistent love, encouragement, and appreciation. We can still listen to them with our hearts.

190

Mimi Brodsky Chenfield *received a B.A. in sociology from Russell Sage College and an M.A. in education from the State University of New York at Oneonta. She began teaching in 1956 and since then has worked with people of all ages from New York to Hawaii. In Columbus, Ohio, where she now lives, she is a member of numerous arts and education councils. She has published several poems, articles, and books and has received many awards for her contributions to education and the arts. She and her husband, Howard, have three children and seven grandchildren.*

Children have never been very good at
listening to their elders, but they have
never failed to imitate them.

—JAMES BALDWIN
Nobody Knows My Name: More Notes of a Native Son

Rona Leichter Seidel

Help Your Children
Reach for the Stars

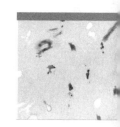

Being a parent is the most important—
*and probably the most demanding—*job you will ever have.
To get the job, you don't need a degree or a license, you don't even have
to fill out an application. But once you take on the job, you'll have it for
a lifetime, and in spite of a bewilderingly vast body of literature on the
subject, you'll most likely have to figure this job out for yourself as you
go. Fortunately, however, there are a host of us who have struggled with
similar jobs. All of us are different and all of our children are different,
but those of us who have already raised kids, taught them, or worked
with them in some other capacity have all learned a few things that we

would like to pass on to other parents. Here are a few thoughts that may help make the job of parenting a little less demanding and a little more productive.

It is okay to say no! Set boundaries for your children and do not worry about what relatives or other parents will do or think. You must do what you are comfortable doing. Parenting is not a popularity contest. Your children do want rules—they will feel more secure and have fewer worries when you provide guidelines for them to follow. Allow decision-making at age-appropriate levels, but don't expect to run your family as a democracy. As a teacher, I do not run my classroom democratically—I set the rules. Parents need to do the same. A structured environment leaves less room for confusion. Let your children know your expectations, and encourage them to strive to meet high goals.

Don't be afraid of making mistakes. We all make them. Let your kids know that from time to time you have made wrong decisions and that they will, too. Help them see that the fear of making mistakes sometimes causes us to hold back and miss out on opportunities to learn. When your children make mistakes, encourage them to talk about what they have learned and what they might do differently next time.

Support your child's teachers. If you disagree with a teacher's decision or think a teacher has acted inappropriately in some way, speak to the teacher by phone, in person, or by written note. Listen to both sides before you reach your conclusions. Good teachers are always willing to listen to a parent's perspective, but they need time to present their side too.

Don't do your child's homework. You have completed your schooling; your child has not. If you don't make your child responsible for school assignments, he or she won't learn to be independent. I once had a student who looked at me in disbelief when he saw his poor grade on an assignment— he had been sure his housekeeper was smart enough to achieve a higher score! Teach responsibility by expecting your children to do their own chores, and do not make excuses for them if they don't complete the work. Allow them to accept the consequences, while helping with time constraints and organization skills.

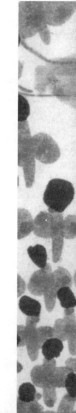

Allow your child to stumble. I have yet to teach the perfect child. Let your children know that you will still love them if they bring home a disappointing grade.

Make homework home *work.* The emphasis is on home. Encourage your son or daughter to do homework in the same place at approximately the same time each day. Sit nearby and do your own work or read a book. Make this a stress-free time.

Do not compare! Each child learns in different ways and at a different pace, even children within a family unit. Do not compare your children with one another, or with their cousins, or with the neighbors' kids.

Create memories each day. Take lots of pictures, keep scrapbooks, and cherish your kids' junk. If your child is a collector, make room for those "valuables." Display creative work with pride. Isn't this the reason for refrigerators? Don't forget that grandparents have refrigerators, too! Your kids will be thrilled to see their artwork displayed on Nana and Papa's fridge.

Listen to your children. It is amazing what you can learn during carpool if you keep your ears open. The kids don't suspect you are hearing their chatter because they think you are busy driving. But even better, when you are alone with your child in the car, you both have a captive audi-

> **"***It is amazing what you can learn during carpool if you keep your ears open.***"**

ence. Here is a ripe opportunity for honest, down-to-earth discussion. I shudder to think how much of that time my children and I spent arguing about which radio station played the "right" music. If I only knew then what I know now! I see kids dropped off at my school each morning without a good-bye because Mom or Dad is engrossed in a phone conversation. Put the cell phones away until the kids are out of the car. We teachers like to see the lucky children who get out of the car giggling or singing because of the fun they have just had with Mom or Dad. These kids are ready for a wonderful day ahead.

Talk with your children. Once or twice a week make dinnertime special. No television, no homework, no newspaper. Talk about the day or the week. Have each person, young and old, tell about something nice that he or she did for someone else, about something fun they did during the week, or about something interesting they learned. This may become such an enjoyable time that you'll all want to do it more often. Don't keep an eye on the clock. Forget about that good program about to be shown on television, the one you think you cannot miss. When your children grow up and set out on their own, there will be too much time to watch television.

Teach your children to be charitable. Do good deeds together. When our kids were young, they joined us when we volunteered at a shelter for homeless women. Our children were aware that we wrote checks to charitable institutions, but they did not relate to this act. Spending the night at the shelter and serving dinner and breakfast to the ladies there made our kids more aware of the needs of others less fortunate than our family. Hopefully, as adults, they will now involve themselves in the doing of good deeds. Within my classroom, we work on projects such as the collection of canned goods for the flood-weary residents of Honduras. I recall one student who visited an assisted-living home on a regular basis with his mom. He was always excited about the visits, and he looked forward to the positive reinforcement he knew he would receive from the aging adults. What pleasure he must have brought them, too!

Count your blessings every day. You are so lucky to have the important job of being a parent. Enjoy the time you spend together with your sons and daughters. This time is so precious, and so fleeting. Cherish their beauty and their thoughts. Listen to them, praise them, comfort them. Don't ever stop hugging them. And don't be afraid. Just set your goals high, help your children to reach for the stars, and may all your dreams come true.

Rona Leichter Seidel *was born in Newark, New Jersey, and received her bachelor's degree from Hofstra University in 1963 and her master's from Mercer University in 1979. She has taught elementary school for almost thirty years, the majority of which she has spent in Atlanta. Rona and her husband, Barry, have three children and almost three grandchildren at this writing. She enjoys traveling around the world, reading, and needlework.*

Parentage is a very important
profession, but no test of fitness
for it is ever imposed in the
interest of the children.

—GEORGE BERNARD SHAW

Richard Wagner

The Wisdom of Our Traditions

It is only twenty-five years since I was *appointed a school principal,* but my career in education has drawn on four thousand years of Jewish life and letters. My experiences are therefore rooted in a particular tradition, but some of its insights speak to parents from all traditions.

I want simply to convey three important truths that are grounded in centuries of Jewish wisdom. They have helped generations of parents nurture their children.

You should teach your child to be a person of the book. The written word—the Jewish art form—is the vitality of the Jewish people. It can also enliven parents and children from every other culture.

Parents need to be book people. Their children will learn from their example that immersion in wise and humane literature can provide both insight for living and heroes and heroines to emulate.

Read with your children and learn together about your own heritage, whether religious or cultural. A scholar whom I have always admired once told me two things. First, read the life of Lincoln. Not only was he the greatest American president, but he also represented the finest of American values. Second, study at least one *Mishna* (passage of rabbinic law) a day. Daily immersion in the body of teachings handed down in your tradition should become a habit. What you learn in this exercise will not necessarily be as important as the discipline that such regular reading enforces. Open the book every day.

> **"Fixing the world is not only an activity but also an attitude."**

You should inspire your children to fix the world. We are citizens of a global village, and we have inherited a world threatened by ethical and ecological catastrophe. The ancient call to the Jewish people was "to repair the world as the Almighty's kingdom has ordered it." This is a worthy call for every people. Rabbi Arthur Green tells us that "we have to help fix a broken world. We have *Mitzvot* [good deeds] to do, including especially those of relieving suffering and injustice that keep so many of our fellow humans from seeing the image of God in themselves and others."

Fixing the world is not only an activity, but also an attitude. Recently, a student of mine was inspired to do some world-fixing. She collected more than three hundred stuffed animals from her schoolmates, cleaned them, repaired them, and gave them away to children in shelters for the abused and homeless. Her creative act of kindness manifested her consistent disposition to help others. Teach your children that when we provide examples of fixing the world, we can change lives—especially our own!

Help your child become a Mentsh.

The Yiddish word *Mentshlichkeit* refers to the quality of being humane. This quality is hard to define, but an anonymous Jewish writer has described it as well as anyone.

> The finest thing you can say about a man is that he is a *Mentsh.*

> To be a *Mentsh* has nothing do with success, wealth or status.

> The key to being a real *Mentsh* is nothing less than character:

> Rectitude, dignity, a sense of what is right and responsible.

In Jewish tradition, being a *Mentsh* is the fulfillment of a divine imperative to live in a godly manner and to behave (if it were possible) as God would act. In every tradition, the ideal of *Mentshlichkeit* can remind both parents and children that the noblest aspiration is to be a man or woman of character.

As parents, we should know and pass on the wisdom of our traditions to our children. We should not lose sight of the large and important issues. If we can convey these three messages—to be a person of the book, to fix the world, and to be a *Mentsh*—many of our more mundane and trivial concerns will take care of themselves.

Richard Wagner *is a native of Wheeling, West Virginia, and he holds a Ph.D. degree from Columbia Pacific University. Richard has been involved in education for more than twenty-five years, both as a teacher and as a consultant for adult education groups. He currently is headmaster of the Greenfield Hebrew Academy in Atlanta, and in this capacity received the Hero in Jewish Education award in 1999. He and his wife, Marcia, who is also a teacher, have three children.*

199

Sheila Freundlich Mofson

Building a Person of Merit

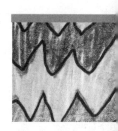

My daughters were already eight and ten years old when I began my career as a private piano teacher. This was the ideal occupation for a mother of two school-aged children: I was at home when my children came home from school. They knew not to disturb me, but my presence there was comforting to them and to me. In the first years of my profession I taught as many as fifty piano students per week, one at a time—the equivalent of a full-time job.

As my husband and I raised our daughters and as I worked with a wide variety of students and parents, I learned some things that I would like to pass on to a new generation of parents.

Respect your child's needs. From the first stages of their lives, children have all the same needs as adults—the needs for love, admiration, and guidance, for learning and achievement.

Always consider what you do or say, for you are an example to your children, whether you want to be or not. Children are continuously learning at an extraordinary rate. They are constantly absorbing tangible knowledge as well as intangible values and behaviors from their elders. They learn as much from unspoken comportment and example as from expressed values.

Have consistently high expectations and clearly delineate what those expectations are. Don't harp on things that you consider less important. Try to give your children space, but at the same time, never back off from the important issues. When my children were older, our rule of thumb involving curfews, for instance, was that they could stay out late at night, but if they changed locations they had to call us so we always knew where they were. We also called them when we were away from home so they always knew how to reach us if they needed to. They never took advantage of our flexible rules because we treated them as responsible adults.

Don't overload children with too many after-school activities. Children work very hard in school all day and after school, participating in sports and clubs and doing their homework. They need to have time to be children and to play. Kids learn many things from playing and relaxing. Sometimes unstructured time is as valuable as structured activities. Becoming adept at a few things builds more confidence than dabbling in many things.

Always give children very specific directions. They are often confused if they are left with too many choices. Children don't understand subtle messages and innuendoes. They usually think about things in a very specific way. In piano teaching, I always try to apply that rule by starting with what a child already knows and understands and building from there. I try to break down physical skills or facts to the smallest components and teach them one component at a time. I never add the next skill until the first is understood and absorbed, and I constantly review old skills.

Show your children when you are pleased with them. If they know how to please us, they will strive to do that. If they are unsure of what we expect, or believe it is too difficult, they will give up.

Become familiar with and take into consideration the stages of learning as explored by Jean Piaget, the great educator. By being cognizant of what your children are able to understand, you will know what to expect of them and not expect too much or too little.

Encourage children often. As parents and educators we need to consider our primary job that of building self-confidence that will last a lifetime. A wonderful way to teach skills and self-confidence is always, always to say something good first—even if you have to search for something positive to say. In my piano teaching I sometimes resorted to "You really like that piece, don't you?" or "You sat up straight and tall for the whole song." After building up a child's confidence by saying something positive, you can correct mistakes. Home recitals or art shows or dramatic readings are good confidence builders. Invite friends and family members, serve refreshments, and lavish lots of honest praise on the performer.

Never lie to children. They will not believe you this time or any time after that. Don't compliment your child falsely. He or she will know you are lying.

Listen to your children attentively. Try to understand the meaning of their spoken and their unspoken words. Good communication requires your complete attention. Take children seriously. Never be condescending to them. Their level of behavior and understanding may not be as mature as yours, but it is as important.

Encourage your children to talk with you about anything that is bothering them. Rebellious behavior is often a manifestation of insecurity. Children rebel for many reasons. They may feel their parents' or their teachers' expectations are too high and are unattainable, or they may feel that expectations are too low and that they are not getting the respect they deserve. Children need independence and may feel smothered by rules and restrictions, or they may feel they have too much

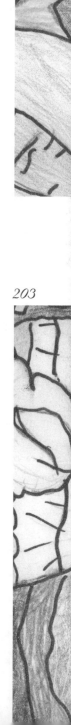

independence and that their parents don't care enough about them. They may be angry at us, or they may feel inferior. Urge them to discuss their feelings with you, and listen when they do.

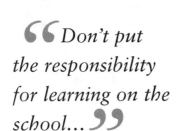

66 *Don't put the responsibility for learning on the school...* **99**

Be involved in whatever your child is learning. In my studio, parents attend lessons and supervise home practice until their children are mature and self-motivated enough to work alone. Don't put the responsibility for learning on the school, the church or synagogue, the leader, or the instructor. Parents and teachers must form a partnership in the learning process. Without that mutual cooperation and understanding, progress will be spotty at best and nonexistent at worst. Never contradict your child's tutor when your child is present. Save that for a telephone call when your child is not at home.

Be aware of the importance of your child's study and practice time. Phones should not interrupt (that's what answering machines are for), TVs and stereos should not interfere with concentration, and other siblings should learn to respect that dedicated time.

Find a central location where your children can study or practice at home. Avoid stationing them in a basement or another remote location. Don't let your children see study or practice as a punishment, but rather as a daily activity that fits comfortably into family life. Children will resist and resent having to practice or study if it takes them out of the mainstream. Don't let your children feel isolated when they are working.

Don't prejudge your child. Children respond to your expectations or to your lack of confidence in them. I do not screen potential students by perceived ability or

so-called "talent." Every child is capable of learning—some more slowly than others—but all children can learn and achieve within their individual capacity.

Your goals—and your child's teacher's goals—should be to appreciate the skills your child is learning and to build self-confidence through achievement. Love and respect your child, and you will build a person of merit who loves and respects you and others in return.

Sheila Freundlich Mofson *taught mathematics in her native Brooklyn after receiving her B.A. from Brooklyn College in 1959. She earned her M.A. in music at Syracuse University and has taught piano privately to children for over thirty years, also serving as a music teacher in a local school. She has published three works on reading music and on piano instruction. Sheila and her husband, Edward, live in Syracuse and have two grown children. She also enjoys singing in a women's trio, walking, knitting, and piano accompaniment.*

If a mother respects both herself
and her child from his very first
day onward, she will never need
to teach him respect for others.

—ALICE MILLER

Joel Yager

Patience and Practice:
Lessons about Raising Children

*H*ere *are a few lessons* *I've learned about* *raising children.* Some I learned from my parents, family, teachers, and friends. Others I learned from reading or through personal experience. Some things that I once thought I knew I have had to learn all over again. Raising children calls for patience and practice to get things right, or at least to get them better.

Show your children respect. Children, like everyone else, have a lot of pride, and that pride is easily hurt. Never talk down to them. Never humiliate them. Never embarrass them in front of other people. Look for ways to compliment them, to say something nice to and about them. You probably like to be treated that way, too.

Listen carefully to them. Let them know that they can look to you when they need to get something off their chest. Learn to be silent when they are telling you about their problems. (The advice can come later.) Listen also when they want to share everyday experiences with you. The better you listen, the more they will want to share their lives with you.

Teach your children to be tolerant and not "tribal." Show them how to appreciate all good people in every community, whether local or global. They can learn from you that it is better not to attach themselves to groups with narrow and intolerant views.

Encourage them to share credit for their accomplishments. Almost all the good things we achieve depend on the help of others. Teach your children to appreciate the contributions of others and to acknowledge their help with a word of thanks whenever possible. It's good for children to learn that all of us must rely on each other. It's even better when they can be openly grateful for the help that others give.

Help them find a balance between caution and trust. Although you may want them to like people in general, help them realize that some people will take advantage of them. On the other hand, teach them that people who never trust others miss out on the best things in life, like friendships, love, and intimacy.

Encourage your children to invest time and effort in a few good friends. A few deep friendships are worth more than a lot of superficial acquaintances. Being popular may seem like fun for a short while, but it will never feel as good as having real friendships.

Never set your children in competition with one another. Parents should help children bond with each other and develop deep, lifelong friendships.

Teach your children to use their time well. Although they should know that wasting time is often fun and sometimes necessary, they also need to realize that they must use their time wisely when they want to accomplish something. Patience, diligence, and persistence are valuable tools, and your children will need them more and more as they grow older.

Help them learn more about what they naturally feel curious about or feel drawn to. Help them find opportunities that enhance their natural abilities instead of forcing them to do things they're not really suited for. Help them nurture and practice their talents. Teach children that even the most talented people need to work hard, practice, strive for excellence, and take pride in the quality of what they do.

Encourage your children to aim high. Help them develop a long-term vision for what they'd like to accomplish in life and get out of life. Let them know that it's all right to set some goals that may never be totally achieved. That way they will be continue to be challenged, engaged, and stimulated throughout adulthood.

Seek help from a caring teacher or counselor if your child displays emotional or behavioral problems. When parents face difficulties with their children, they often need an experienced person to listen to them, to help them communicate better with each other, or to help them establish and enforce rules of proper conduct within the family. Serious emotional problems may require psychological or medical help. Don't wait too long.

Tell your children how much you love them as often as you can, and give them the emotional and practical support they need as they grow from one stage to another. Hug them a lot even after they become adults. And show them that you as parents also love each other. They can learn from you what it means to form loving relationships.

Give your children a strong faith even if you feel that you will never really know the nature of God. If you teach that God's purpose for them is to learn, to make things better, and to help other people, you probably won't go wrong.

Joel Yager *was born in the Bronx and received his B.S. from City College of New York and his M.D. from Albert Einstein College of Medicine. He is professor of psychiatry at the University of New Mexico School of Medicine and is professor emeritus in the Department of Psychiatry and Behavioral Sciences at UCLA School of Medicine. Joel's research has focused, among other issues, on eating disorders, primary care aspects of psychiatry, family therapy, and stress. He has written and edited, by himself and with others, more than 200 articles and seven books, including SPECIAL PROBLEMS IN THE MANAGEMENT OF EATING DISORDERS. He and his wife, Eileen, a pediatrician, have two children, each of whom is also a doctor.*

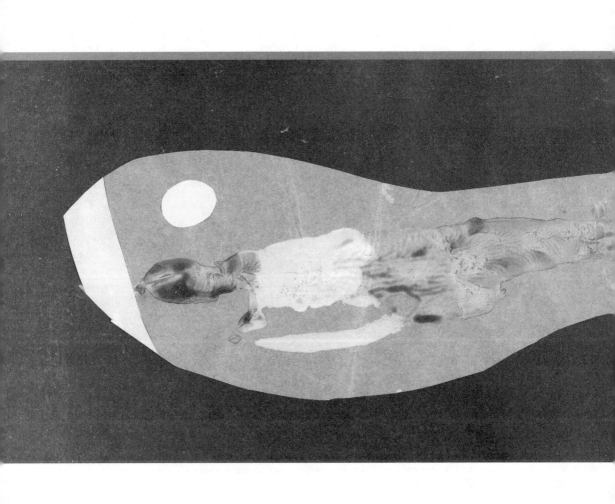

Kay E. Johnson

You Are the Adult

After almost forty years as a mother, a volunteer in the schools, an English teacher, and a remedial reading teacher, I have observed a wide variety of children in many different settings. I have had the opportunity to try out various approaches—some rewarding and some disappointing—on my own children and my students, and I have also watched the successes and failures of other teachers and parents as they worked with children. I offer here a short list of some things to remember as you raise your child, some guidelines and attitudes that I feel have passed the test of time and experience and that should be valuable to any parent.

Act like an adult. As the parent, you are the adult.

Don't strive to be your child's "friend." Friendship between you and your child will evolve after a loving, respectful, and trusting relationship is established.

Come up with a clear and realistic idea of what you expect from your child at each stage of his or her development. Make sure your child understands the expectations and what the consequences will be if the expectations aren't met. Then be consistent!

Establish limits. Children both need and want discipline.

Praise your child. Children need realistic—that is, "earned"—praise for work toward and achievement of goals.

Be flexible, creative, and enthusiastic when dealing with your children.

As someone once said, give your children roots and wings. Give them family and structure to hold onto, but instill in them the confidence to go out on their own.

Be firm but never abusive.

Allow children to suffer the consequences of their behavior and choices.

Teach responsibility at all ages.

Allow your children the joy of discovery.

Be the example.

Offer your child reasonable choices, and then require commitment once your child makes a choice.

Guide and help your children, but don't do their tasks for them.

Make books, art, music, and religion a vital part of their lives.

Expect respect from your children.

Give your children unconditional love.

Following everything on this list will not, of course, guarantee smooth sailing through all your parenting days. But if you provide for your children a sound sense of direction, a sense of the joy that lies ahead in the journey, and a loving and safe home port, you will weather the stormy days together, and one day they will be ready to take the helm themselves.

Kay E. Johnson *received her B.A. in English from Mercer University in 1960. She has been a devoted teacher of English and reading and a school volunteer for over thirty years. Kay's love of children and her creative ways of reaching kids have been hallmarks of her career. She and her husband, Tom, also a contributor to this volume, have two children and two granddaughters, and are looking forward to the arrival of their first grandson.*

213

It is the function of parents
to see that their children habitual-
ly experience the true consequences
of their conduct.

—HERBERT SPENCER
Education: Intellectual, Moral, and Physical

Polly P. Hart

The Big Picture
(and Some Small Stuff)

Parenting is an impossible task—
unrealistic expectations, lots of work, long hours, no pay.
And we'd better do it right, because everyone is watching us to see
how our children turn out.

Nevertheless, most of us come to the task of child rearing with
high hopes and ideals. We look upon an infant as a blank slate ready
to be filled in. As members of a democratic society, it is natural for us
to expect that providing equal opportunity will result in equal real-
ization of potential. We presume that if we provide the appropriate
care and nurturing to our children during their early years, their
potential will unfold as they mature. Conversely, we believe that if

those early years are troubled and lacking in proper care, much of a child's potential will never be realized.

But what we often fail to take into account is the fact that our children come to us not as blank slates, but rather as bundles of biologically determined constraints wrapped in layers of potential. Even when we provide just the right amount of nurturing, just the right mix of guidance and encouragement, and the loftiest of hopes and dreams for our children, that bundle of constraints—that genetically determined core of intelligence, temperament, health, and personality—makes itself known, helping to form our children's identity, sometimes in unpredictable ways. Our children are from us and through us, but they may not be *like* us. They may not even resemble our image of what we thought they should be.

It is hard for some of us to accept this fact about child rearing. Too often we need our kids to be a particular type of someone. As long as our child matches our ideal, things go smoothly. When our child's needs do not fit with our own needs, conflicts arise. Family counselors and child psychologists constantly see problems that result from a poor fit between parents' and children's needs.

When raising children, we simply don't know how much influence our nurturing will have on them—how much we can change and how much we can't change. Nature will play an important role in determining who our children become, in spite of all our efforts at nurturing. Barring trauma or brain pathology, genetics will probably win out in determining who our children become. But family culture and style will determine how much conflict will occur as our children are growing up.

Our challenge, then, as parents is finding ways to guide our children with a minimum of struggle against their biological constraints, ways to allow our children's potential to unfold smoothly, and ways to balance our own needs against those of our children. Nurture does not have to be a battle against nature. As impossible as the task of parenting may seem at times, we can find ways to minimize the difficulties and maximize the joys. I offer here a list of suggestions that may help as you engage in that most impossible of tasks, raising a child.

Make health and safety your priority. All things can be worked out in time if you can get your kids to age twenty-one safe and sound!

Pay attention to what kids do right. Let them make mistakes.

Examine your lifestyle. Kids require time and energy in goodly amounts. Both parents working is not the problem. It's both parents working in jobs that take all their time and energy.

Know your kids' friends.

Be all that you can be, but don't try it when your kids are growing up.

Let children have their own dreams.

Fill your home with all kinds of books and music.

Consider cutting back if your job leaves you chronically stressed and irritable. A family needs time for play and relaxation.

Laugh often.

Take the long view.

Let your children know how you decide things by thinking out loud when they are listening.

Help children learn to view with a critical eye the messages delivered to them constantly by sophisticated marketing techniques. Don't let them trade quality of life for a quantity of stuff.

When they are old enough, have children cook (or help cook) weekly.

Spend time away from your kids.

Don't tolerate put-downs or bragging.

Teach kids about money—real finances, not just allowances.

Insist on respectful language.

Consider thoughtfulness and consideration for others more important than perfect behavior.

Have kids do their own laundry after age eleven.

Learn computers from your kids.

Discuss current events, politics, sex, and religion with them.

Invite your children to help you help the less fortunate.

Interfere with "all or nothing" thinking.

Don't fret about missed meals, staying up late, teen fads, or Twinkies.

Deal with messy rooms once weekly or less. Respect your children's privacy but clean their rooms on occasion.

Encourage time with grandparents.

Don't protect your children unduly from life's difficult times.

Keep laughing!

Complete sex education by seventh grade.

Have dogs and cats. If you have allergies, keep the dogs and cats and take more antihistamines.

Don't expect complete honesty from teens. Well, you can expect it, but good, solid kids do lots of hedging as teens.

Keep a resident "grinch" (the culprit responsible for lost socks and missing report cards).

Know age-appropriate norms.

Say yes a lot.

Know the red flags for alcohol and drugs.

When necessary, refer to the parent grapevine, which knows much but can't remember who said what.

Teach right and wrong.

Demand respect for those who are different.

Have kids master one area of interest or skill outside of school.

Give more hugs than money.

Consider cars for teenagers a privilege.

Seek and support wonderful teachers.

Teach skills for living, such as changing a tire and changing a diaper.

Don't confuse what mass marketing wants you to buy for what your kids actually need.

Pick your battles carefully; hassle and nag as little as possible.

Other than curfew, make rules in response to things your kids screw up rather than anticipating their mistakes.

Learn how to spot problems:

Serious Problem—biologically based psychiatric illness or substance abuse. These problems require professional attention. They are ongoing conditions that you can learn to manage.

Potentially Serious Problem That Can Get Worse—anxiety, depression, attention and learning problems in school, or chronically unacceptable behavior. These problems can be helped. Don't wait to look for and ask for advice and assistance!

Conflict That Feels Serious But Isn't—This kind of problem is often the result of a particular parenting style that doesn't fit a particular youngster. Find other ways of approaching the problem or wait till it goes away. Don't worry too much about appearance. Things like body piercing, tattoos, and dyed hair are often an expression of peer culture. If forty-year-olds don't do it, then this too will pass!

If you're not sure which type of problem you are dealing with, seek advice from someone who works with lots of kids for a living and who has lots of experience.

And finally, work on a sense of confidence that your children can and will find their own way into adulthood, on their own timetable, albeit with false starts, mistakes, and unbelievable folly—just as you did! Children do in fact finally grow up, and relationships with their parents are usually much improved when that happens.

Polly P. Hart *earned her B.A. in religion from Centenary College in 1967 and her master's in social work from Tulane University in 1969. For more than thirty years, Polly has served as a clinical social worker in both the public and private sectors, and she has published a work on the changing biological perspectives on the nature versus nurture debate. She and her husband, Will, have raised three children in a blended family. An ardent hobbyist, Polly enjoys antiquing, gardening, photography, and writing.*

Ethel Seiderman

The Importance of Legacy

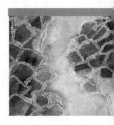

M̃y parents passed on to me the legacy *of many generations.* That legacy explains me, and it is my collected memories that I leave to future generations. My grandsons never tire of hearing how I grew up, of my life at home and school, the pranks I committed, and the stories told me by my parents and grandmother. My early life is the bedrock for my beliefs and values. It led to my commitment to contribute to a better world and my passion for embracing all peoples.

Of course I occasionally have lost my way and succumbed to the glitzy and trendy. But, because I learned who I am, where I came from, and what I have to offer, I am blessed to have been able to give myself wake-up calls.

My brother and I learned that the best life wasn't somewhere else, a wish away, but within our reach. Our parents left us free to design our own destiny, but it had to include making the world better for others as well as for ourselves. We were champions of the underdog and, indeed, were taught that each of us is his brother's keeper.

We learned that all members of a family need to believe that they matter and that their voices are being heard. Unless children feel that they can shape their lives and have influence in directing it, they become disheartened and disillusioned. Family members should be able to count on support and encouragement from their community so they can sprout wings and launch themselves. The children need to learn that they are loved unconditionally, that their families see them as achievers, and that we believe in their specialness and adore them for it. We need to build circles of encouragement and provide the resources so that each child is protected and enabled to excel in his or her chosen direction.

Although each generation must make its own journey, some lessons are well worth passing along for consideration. Some they will embrace, others they will redesign, and still others they will leave along the roadside. But uppermost must be the message that commits each generation to sustaining a peaceful, humane, and caring world. This must resonate from one generation to the next. Harmony, equity, respect, inclusion, and tenderness have no substitutes.

Ethel Seiderman *was born and raised in New York City and currently lives in San Anselmo, California. She received her B.A. degree from Brooklyn College in 1953 and her M.A. from San Francisco State in 1969. In her fifty years of working with children, she has been a classroom teacher as well as an administrator of daycare and early education programs. She has written widely on serving families and children. She was named California Legislative Woman of the Year in 1998 and was included among a list of Women Making History in 1988. Her husband, Stanley, is a social worker. They have two grown children.*

Whenever I held
my newborn baby in
my arms, I used to
think that what I said
and did to him could
have an influence not
only on him but on all
whom he met, not only
for a day or a month or
a year, but for all
eternity—a very, very
challenging and
exciting thought
for a mother.

—ROSE KENNEDY

223

Marshall P. Duke

THIRTY THINGS
I Have Learned about Children
IN THIRTY YEARS
as a Psychologist

KIDS AND THEIR OWN HAPPINESS

1 *Children need not be and cannot be happy all the time.* (This is a corollary of the broader dictum, "No human being will be happy all the time.") Somewhere along the line, we picked up the idea that our children must be happy every moment of every day. We don't want our children to cry—we are uncomfortable when our children cry—because if they cry that will mean they are unhappy. That in turn will mean that we as parents are failing them somehow and that they will grow up to be miserable wretches who will hate us and not care for us in our old age!

2 *Children need not get their way all the time.* Allowing children to get their way all the time does not empower them. On the

contrary, it renders them vulnerable to breakdown when they are faced with the exigencies of the real world where no one gets his or her way all the time and everyone must compromise.

3 *Children do not instinctively know what is best for them.* There are biological and psychological reasons why they are dependent upon us for so many years of their lives. I am amazed when I see parents asking their young children which food they want, where they want to go for vacation, what clothes they want, or what shows they want to see, especially when the parents are not in fact open to some of the options the child may select. Further, parents who bend over backwards to get everything a child wants are planting a cruel time bomb in that child's garden. When the child goes out into the real world, there will be no such unconditional and unidirectional accommodation of his or her wants. Train your child to observe certain limits and give your child guidance in making choices. Negotiations, compromises, and frustrations will be the order of the day. Every child needs to be ready to deal with them.

4 *Sooner or later, despite all efforts to the contrary, every parent hurts his or her child.* Almost all of us can remember times when things our parents said or did as we were growing up hurt us. When we become parents, we are determined to avoid doing anything that we think might hurt our own children. Life, however, is too complex and filled with too many ambiguous situations for parents to do exactly the right thing at the right time throughout the eighteen years or so a child remains under their wing. Furthermore, no parent can possibly foresee the effects of his or her reactions or decisions on a given child at a given time. Get to know your child's needs and limitations as well as you can, do your best to make fair and appropriate decisions in each situation, and then don't worry that you might make a mistake now and then.

5 *All children will have their feelings hurt.* Some will have their feelings hurt a lot! First, the older children get, the more unsupervised time they spend with other children. By nature, children are less inhibited in what they say, and they often do not spare the feelings of others. This is not always a bad

thing, mind you. Many a child who has endured unkind words, taken them to heart, and changed behavior that was alienating them from their peers has had a brighter future because of what they learned from those unpleasant experiences. Second, no parent can possibly control all the things that happen to children when they are away from home—in schools, on playgrounds, in buses, at camp. Parents who try to ensure that their children are never hurt emotionally are setting an impossible course.

6 *Children need to learn how to deal with being hurt.* Parents should help their children find ways to cope with painful or unpleasant experiences. This may sometimes involve such "unhealthy" things as kicking balls, breaking (useless) things, screaming, drawing angry pictures and tearing them up, writing angry letters that are never mailed, or other similar activities that might help the child release his or her anger and frustration without hurting anyone.

7 *Manners and social graces count for children too.* It is not for the world to accommodate to the idiosyncrasies of our children. In a society that is civil and functional, each member must accommodate to the needs of the community. This does not mean sacrificing individuality, it means that we agree to act in civil ways with each other and not demand everything we want exactly when we want it. Spoiled kids may be happy in the eyes of their parents, but the inability to accommodate to the needs of others is another one of those time bombs that will explode when the child hits the real world.

KIDS AND PARENTS

8 *Parents must nurture their own relationship.* It is the Foundation (with a capital *F*) of the family structure. It's good for children to see parents going out together, traveling together, buying gifts for each other, and showing that they care for one another. It's also good for children to know that their parents can argue, even be unkind to each other, and get over it. Children will learn forgiveness and commitment to relationships by observing these ideals in their parents' lives.

9 *Divorce is rarely if ever the "best thing for children."* When two people agree to marry and care for one another, they are making a serious commitment to becoming a family. But when they agree to have children and raise them together, they are upping considerably the stakes on their family commitment. No marriage is perfect. Problems are bound to arise in the best of families. Compromises are a necessity, not a nicety. Divorce as a solution to marriage difficulties is so far down from whatever is above it on the list that it should not be considered until all other measures have been exhausted. One reason why children of divorced parents have higher rates of divorce themselves is that they see divorce as an option.

We owe our children a secure and relatively stable place to grow in. The line about "doing what's best for the children" is typically a rationalization from two adults who have accepted the fact that "children need not be and cannot be happy all the time," while conveniently forgetting the adjunct principle, "adults need not be and cannot be happy all the time." Parents' responsibility to their children goes beyond their own individual needs.

10 *Parents must treat their own parents with love and respect.* How sad it is to have to say this, but all too often children grow in a family where grandparents are seen as problems or burdens. To this I can only say one thing: From the way you treat your aging parents, your children will learn how to treat their aging parents. Treat your parents (and elderly folks in general) in exactly the same way you want to be treated, because that is what is going to happen. Want to live in a home? Want to be visited once a week for an hour? Want to be talked about behind your back, to be ridiculed? You can make it happen!

11 *Consistency in dealing with children is not necessarily a virtue.* As Emerson once said, "A foolish consistency is the hobgoblin of little minds." No parent can possibly be consistent all the time; no two parents can always agree on all the things that they do with their children. The best we can hope for is actually something very positive from the perspective of the child, and that is to be "consistently and reliably inconsistent." By this I mean that children will learn, for example, that "when Mom is angry, she will never agree to let me go to Mary's house; I need to wait until she calms down." Learning to spot consistent inconsistencies is

the key to being able to deal with the same phenomena in the real world. Nothing is always. Nothing is never. Children need to learn how to recognize inconsistencies in the real world and how to alter their behavior to deal with them.

12 *Kids cannot tell the difference between "quality time with parents" and "time with parents."* The concept of quality time seems to have been invented as a justification for guiltlessly minimizing parental contact and responsibility. Any parents who have discussed with their grown children the special things that the children remember from childhood know that rarely will the children mention the things that the parents felt were "quality time." No one can tell when a very simple moment will turn into a memory or experience with lifelong impact. The more time you spend with your kids when they are young, the more likely it is that one of these important moments will occur. I can't wait until the concept of quality time leaves our vocabulary.

KIDS AND OTHER PEOPLE

13 *No two children ever have the same parents, even in the same family.* The parents of a firstborn child are completely new at child rearing, and they behave accordingly. The parents of a second child have already had some experience in child-raising, and they will behave accordingly. The picture changes slightly with each addition of another child to the family mix.

Moreover, the temperament and personality of each child help determine the ways their parents treat them. An easy, affable child produces and has very different parents than does a difficult, obstreperous youngster. It is thus impossible to treat all children exactly alike; stop trying to do so. Treat them as fairly as possible within the confines of the relationship they and you have established with one another. Although fairness and equal treatment are fine and good goals, it is impossible to achieve them all the time (or even most of the time). Having trouble believing this? Ask one of your siblings to describe his or her perceptions of your parents; you might be amazed that you are talking about the same people.

14 *When two kids get into an argument, they can usually thrash it out themselves.* Parents should never take up children's disagreements at the adult level. Adults stay angry at each other far longer than kids do. Kids are usually back being friends in a matter of days or hours, whereas the parents might find themselves embroiled in the start of a feud that could go on for years. Adult interference in children's disagreements does not further the children's friendship.

15 *Don't insist that children be friends with kids they do not want to be friendly with.* Never force a child to sleep over at a friend's house, because you think it will be "good" for him or her. More times than not, the child will have a bad time and then it will be even harder to get a friendship going.

16 *Some kids want and need a lot of friends.* Other kids want and need a few friends. Some kids want and need no friends at all. Don't force your perception of their need for friends onto your children. In the first place, what you do yourself and what you say may differ. If you have only a couple of close friends, it doesn't make sense to tell your kids that they need lots of friends. Most parents find that their children want and need as many friends as they (the parents) do. In the second place, your child probably knows how many friends he or she wants. Real acceptance of a child means to respect his or her wishes with regard to friends. As parents and teachers, we seem to have become obsessed with the idea that having friends means being happy and successful. How many examples of the wrongness of this idea would you like to hear?

17 *Children can learn to be kind if they see their parents and peers doing kind things.* They cannot learn to be kind by being forced into doing "kind" things they do not want to do. You cannot legislate kindness. Be a good role model instead. Over time, your being kind to others will translate into your children being kind as well.

KIDS AND SCHOOL

18 *Not all kids can do well in school if they try harder or the teachers are good or the food is healthier or if they are not picked on or if they have the right clothes or if their parents help them with their homework.* The fact is that the "Lake Wobegon Effect" is a hoax. There is no place where all the children are above average. Some kids will do better in school than others. Others, no matter how hard they try, will not do as well as this first group of "some kids." This doesn't mean that kids should not try to maximize their performance, but they should not (nor should their parents) feel bad about themselves because they are in the middle of the pack. One of the jobs of parents is to help kids try out as many "packs" as possible so that each child can find a "pack" where he or she is closer to the top! We all know the story about Einstein's being weak in some school subjects, don't we? We all know that the singer, Cher, is dyslexic. What if her parents had their hearts set on her becoming a journalist? All kids need not go to college. All kids cannot be star athletes. All kids cannot play musical instruments well. We are a species composed of people with widely varying skills. As parents, our jobs are to try to fit the foot of the child with one of the many shoes the world offers. How would you feel if you went to a shoe store and found that they carried only one size shoe and that you simply had to wear that size or do without?

19 *Children do not need to hear their parents criticizing their teachers.* Parents must support teachers, at least within earshot of their children. There is little more damaging to the crucial relationship between teacher and child than a parent who openly challenges the teacher's authority. I would add here that, first, no teacher enters the profession with the express intent of hurting, frustrating, or confusing children, and, second, no effective teacher can avoid sometimes and inadvertently hurting, confusing, or treating unfairly his or her students. Like parents, teachers are authorities who must make decisions. By definition, decisions involve choosing one of several courses of action. Inevitably, some people (kids and parents) would prefer that the teacher follow one of the other courses of action.

Every time a teacher makes a decision, therefore, it opens up the possibility of making someone unhappy or of convincing someone that the teacher is a hopeless hack. If you do not like the decisions your child's teacher is making, set up a time to talk with the teacher. Meanwhile, support whatever the teacher says to your child. Yes, that's right, have the child do that outrageous amount of homework until you discuss its outrageousness privately with the teacher.

20 *The most important figures, besides parents, in a child's life are his or her teachers.* Not the tennis pro, not the soccer coach, not the best friend next door. The teachers! Whatever happened to teachers like dear old Mrs. Grundy? Why are there fewer and fewer really old and deeply experienced teachers in our schools? Because many of the best of them have found that it is not worth the hassle of being seen as the enemy by so many for so little compensation.

If you really want to know what kind of a child you have, ask his or her teachers from the current and previous school year. Ask the teachers to be honest with you. Wherever these teachers are in strong agreement, you can attribute the characteristics to the child. Where they are in strong disagreement, you can assume that the characteristics they describe are a result of your child's interaction with that particular teacher. Learn from this. A teacher observes your child 180 days a year for six to seven hours a day, in all sorts of situations and under all sorts of conditions. Is there anyone else besides a parent who has that kind of opportunity to get to know your child? Not the pediatrician. Not the psychologist. Not the social worker. We must listen to teachers. They are not the enemy.

KIDS AND SELF-ESTEEM

21 *Self-esteem is not all it's cracked up to be.* Once, just once, I would like to see a study that shows that self-esteem is related in an actual causal (not correlational) manner to all the good things in the world that it is supposed to be related to. We as parents try so hard to head off jolts to our kids' self-esteem, yet most of our upbringing did not include parental obsession with our self-esteem. How come most of us have grown up to be relatively successful and basically content? (And there is research to back up this statement.)

22 *Empty praise cannot create self-esteem in your child.* When we try to build up kids' self-esteem and expect them to believe that they are good at something just because we say so, we are undermining our own credibility. Kids can see right through this kind of bumper-sticker mentality. They are not dumb. They can look and see that some kids are better runners than they are, some are better in math, others can sing better. When we tell them that they are just as good as everyone else at doing certain things when we know they are not, kids begin (rightly) to disbelieve us. Our praise becomes meaningless to them, and they no longer look at us as reliable. They will take our perfunctory self-esteemisms with a large grain of salt and look elsewhere for self-affirmation. (And we might not like the elsewhere that they look.)

23 *The single most powerful source of self-esteem—for children and adults—is doing something you thought you could not do and doing it pretty well in your own eyes.* Think this through. Doing something you know you can do? No big deal. Doing something that you think you can't do? Impressive to yourself and to others. Deciding on your own that this is good? A real ego builder. But being told you are good because you did something simple? Or even worse, being told you are good even though you really could not or did not do the thing you tried? Who are these adults kidding?

24 *Failure does not destroy self-esteem.* Failure is a signal that a person has not yet mastered the level in which he or she is currently operating. When children fail, they need to stick with the level they are working on, master it, pack away the well-earned self-esteem, and only then look toward something harder. Remember, kids are not dumb. They know when they are not doing something well, especially when they can see other kids their age succeeding at the task. Imagine knowing you have failed at something and then being told by the self-esteem dispensers that you did great and that you should move to the next level.

Do you know who I respect immensely? The karate instructors. They will not give a yellow belt to a kid who has not mastered the skills involved, even if the kids cry, even if the parents beg, even if the child's self-esteem is running on empty. Why? Because they know—and you will see this too if you watch carefully—that when the child masters the required skills (through concerted effort) and earns the belt, the child's face, posture, and way of walking demonstrate a level of self-esteem that no one could instill through skirting the truth.

KIDS AND THEIR NEEDS

25 *Every child must have at least one space that is totally his or hers to control completely.* While it is reasonable for parents to ask that children maintain a sense of order and cleanliness in the public areas of the house, the child's room needs to be monitored on a less stringent standard. While slovenliness and disregard for basic human dignity need not be tolerated, children should be allowed to have some private space and private time without parental constraints.

26 *All kids need exercise for their bodies and for their brains.* Physical exercise is important, but those children who are shy and socially insecure need not feel compelled to play team sports. Individualized sports like karate, weightlifting, long-distance running, and long-distance swimming can provide the needed physical activity without the social stress. Never force a socially uncomfortable child into a team sport if he or she resists. Staying with it will not help; in the long run the child will be even more shy and resentful. However, do force children (if you can) to take music lessons and make them practice. There are countless people who regret that their families gave in to them too easily and allowed them to stop lessons. Similarly, there are countless others who can play instruments as adults and who thank their parents for not letting them quit. Music, dance, or art lessons are good things for adults to have had when they are children. They may not seem to the children like the best things at the time, but see Rules 1 and 2!

27 *Kids love rituals.* They like to do the same things at the same places at the same times of year. Rituals help to define the unique qualities of our families and lives. Giving Dad the same pair of socks every year on his birthday may seem silly, but it is a memory that the family holds on to. Rituals impart stability and predictability to an otherwise (and normally) unpredictable world. Family rituals—

234

foods eaten on holidays, certain outfits worn for special occasions, songs sung together year after year—help children to feel secure. Don't just depend on cultural or religious rituals; invent some that belong to you and your family.

28 *Kids need family mealtimes.* Eat together several times a week. No, this doesn't mean eat meals together at a fast food restaurant. This means sitting together at a table in the warmth and security of a home, eating food that someone in the house worked to prepare. This does not mean a lot of work. It is easy to make a pizza at home. Easy to make hot dogs and hamburgers, easy to make salads, macaroni and cheese, or even a peanut butter and jelly sandwich. Do you think that we adults developed the sense and concept of "comfort food" because we had things like roast chicken, meat loaf, mashed potatoes, or chocolate pudding in Styrofoam containers sitting in the back of a van? The things kids eat when they are secure, warm, and feeling loved are the things they will consider comfort food when they grow up. As parents, it's your choice. What foods will comfort your children after you are gone?

29 *Kids need memories, and parents are the makers of memories.* Think about the sorts of things you want your children to have in their memory banks and develop experiences that will fill those banks up. Do you want them to have memories of making cookies with you? Make cookies with them! (See how easy this is?) Do you want them to remember your reading poetry to them? Do you want them to remember doing charitable things? It seems to me that it is not just the doing of things that helps to shape good people—it is the remembering of doing those things. A child who has such things in his or her memory is a better person.

30 *Every child needs a system of moral belief and spirituality. It doesn't matter what religion is practiced or even if the system of belief is a religious one, per se.* Children simply must have a system that will provide them with standards against which to judge their behavior and guidelines that will help them make difficult decisions. Parents must choose for the children when they are young. If the kids want to switch belief systems later, that's fine and dandy. However, it is a

cop-out to raise a child with no system of belief on the premise that the child can later choose what is best for him or her. The child will grow up facing the oncoming winds of life without sails, without a compass. His or her course will be aimless.

31 *Never trust a list of thirty things (or five things or ten things or seven, even) about anything.* First of all, notice that there are thirty-one things on this list! Creating this list represents an effort to highlight specific ideas that seem good to me right now. The list I have presented here is not the same one I would have written before I had children. It is not the one I would have written when my children were younger. It is the list of someone who is now a grandparent of young children. It will change as they and I grow older. This is my best advice right now. I have not followed all of these bits of wisdom and have been sorry for it. In fact, seeing the results of my failure has caused me to incorporate several things into this list.

I have been a teacher, a psychologist, and a parent for nearly a third of a century. I probably know a lot, but I urge you to be careful when you apply anyone's advice to your own children. Do not dare accept all of the things I have written just because I have written them. Everything will not work for everybody. No one is an expert in all things for all times. Not even the experts on TV.

Marshall P. Duke *is currently Charles Howard Candler Professor of Psychology at Emory University. During his three decades at Emory, he has served as director of the University Counseling Center and chair of the Department of Psychology and has won numerous teaching awards. In addition to working clinically with children, he has been a consultant for public and private schools throughout the U.S. and Great Britain. With Dr. Stephen Nowicki, he is coauthor of a textbook on abnormal psychology and two books dealing with social problems in children,* Helping the Child Who Doesn't Fit In *and* Teaching Your Child the Language of Social Success. *Along with his wife and coeditor Sara, he is the proud parent of three children and the ridiculously doting grandparent of Brandon, Alex, Rachel, Jacob, and Shira.*

Conclusion

$\mathcal{N}$o one can offer *a definitive set of guidelines* for raising children. Some of our experts believe in lots of structure, others recommend a great deal of freedom. Some emphasize the need for strict boundaries and limits, while others encourage parents to be less stringent. Some contributors advise setting high standards for children, but some caution that parents should strive to set reachable goals. Some stress the importance of ensuring success, while others speak of the need to allow failure.

There is a wide spectrum of parenting behavior. Parents constantly have to find a comfortable spot along that spectrum. They may settle into that spot for a while, but they must always be ready to shift to another spot in response to changes in their children, in themselves, and in their environment. No single set of rules can apply for all children at all ages and in all circumstances. Children change in many ways as they grow older, and parenting approaches must change, too. Some methods work for a child at one age, but are inappropriate for that child at another age.

To further complicate things, all children, even those in the same family, are different. Some are passive, others are more active; some are outgoing, others are introverted; some are easy-going, others are anxious. Every child calls for different methods of child rearing. In addition, each parent reacts and responds to different children in different ways. Some guidelines work well for some children but not for others. Some methods work well for some parents and not for others.

We also have to remember that not only do parents and the community participate in child rearing, children are also active participants in their own upbringing. Parenting is not a method or a set of behaviors or statements. Parenting is a complex interactive process affected equally by parents, children, and community. Many different approaches to child rearing can work well.

If there are no hard and fast rules and no guaranteed methods for successful child raising, why do some kids clearly come out well while others do not? Why do some parents just seem to be better at this business? We have found only one universal in these varied approaches to raising children. This universal is not a belief, not an approach, not a singular concept like maintaining self-esteem. It is this:

All of our contributors do what they do not only in response to the children they see before them, they do what they do because in their mind's and heart's eyes they also have images of what they would like the children in their care to become. Each time they interact with a child, they respond not to one child, but to two. The first is the child of the present—the child who needs protection and boundaries and guidance. The second is the child of the future—the adult who is confident and independent and able to care about others.

Sometimes we simply must opt for the needs of the future child over the current child. For example, we may decide that the present child must take piano lessons despite his or her protests because we believe that the child of the future will benefit from being able to play an instrument. Other times the child of the present takes priority. We might decide that the future child really doesn't need soccer frustrations in his or her past and defer to the desire of a non-athletic youngster to quit that sport. This dual-child concept helps us place in perspective the differences that we have found among our experts. The content of their advice surely differs, but the intent of their advice is always the same. The more people work with children, the more they are aware that short-term parenting decisions also have long-term effects. Parents—and other people who work with children—must always keep in mind both the present child and the future adult.

Many paths lead to successful parenting, and even detours may at times be quite useful. While our contributors realize that there is no one road to raising children well, they all recognize that each child is actually two children and that the needs of one must never take total precedence over the needs of the other.

In some ways, raising a child is like writing a novel with many chapters. In a good work of fiction, the main characters develop over time and ultimately become real to the reader. Like a successful novel, the one you write as a parent will be complex and filled with dramatic tension—neither totally lighthearted nor unremittingly tragic. We hope the wisdom collected here will help you find a plot line, a theme, and a few subplots for your work. And remember to enjoy the writing. Your story will be like no other, and that is how it was meant to be.

Recommended Reading

We asked each of our contributors to list several books—from how-to guides to inspirational literature to children's stories—that they found helpful in raising their own children or in their work with children. Here is the result.

Indicates a title suggested by more than one contributor.

ADULT BOOKS

ALL I REALLY NEED TO KNOW I LEARNED IN KINDERGARTEN: UNCOMMON THOUGHTS ON COMMON THINGS
Robert Fulghum

BECOMING A FATHER
Stan Seiderman

BEQUEST OF WINGS: A FAMILY'S PLEASURES WITH BOOKS
Annis Duff

BETWEEN PARENT AND CHILD
Haim G. Ginott

BEYOND RITALIN
Stephen W. Garber, Ph.D., Marianne Daniels Garber, Ph.D., and Robyn Freedman Spizman

BLACK FAMILIES IN WHITE AMERICA
Andrew Billingsley

BOYS! SHAPING ORDINARY BOYS INTO EXTRAORDINARY MEN
William Beausay II

THE BOY WHO WOULD BE A HELICOPTER: THE USES OF STORYTELLING IN THE CLASSROOM
Vivian Gussin Paley

BREAKFAST WITH SCOT
Michael Downing

CARING FOR YOUR BABY AND YOUNG CHILD : BIRTH TO AGE FIVE
American Academy of Pediatrics, Edited by Steven P. Shelov, M.D., F.A.A.P. and Robert E. Hannemann, M.D., F.A.A.P.

*CHILD BEHAVIOR: THE CLASSIC CHILDCARE MANUAL FROM THE GESELL INSTITUTE OF HUMAN DEVELOPMENT
Frances L. Ilg., M.D., Louise Bates Ames, Ph.D., and Sydney M. Baker, Ph.D.

CHILDREN MOVING: A REFLECTIVE APPROACH TO TEACHING
PHYSICAL EDUCATION
George Graham, Shirley Ann Holt/Hale, and Melissa Parker

*CHILDREN: THE CHALLENGE
Rudolf Dreikurs, M.D. and Vicki Soltz, R.N.

THE CONFIDENT CHILD: RAISING A CHILD TO TRY, LEARN, AND CARE
Terri Apter, Ph.D.

THE COURAGE TO RAISE GOOD MEN
Olga Silverstein and Beth Rashbaum

DIFFERENT AND WONDERFUL: RAISING BLACK CHILDREN
IN A RACE-CONSCIOUS SOCIETY
Dr. Darlene Powell Hopson and Dr. Derek S. Hopson

*DR. SPOCK'S BABY AND CHILD CARE
Benjamin Spock, M.D. and Stephen J. Parker, M.D.

A FINE YOUNG MAN: WHAT PARENTS, MENTORS, AND EDUCATORS CAN
DO TO SHAPE ADOLESCENT BOYS INTO EXCEPTIONAL MEN
Michael Gurian

FIRST THINGS FIRST: TO LIVE, TO LOVE, TO LEARN, TO LEAVE A LEGACY
Steven Covey, A. Roger Merrill, Rebecca R. Merrill

FULL ESTEEM AHEAD: 100 WAYS TO BUILD SELF-ESTEEM
IN CHILDREN AND ADULTS
Diane Loomans with Julia Loomans

GET OUT OF MY LIFE, BUT FIRST COULD YOU DRIVE ME AND CHERYL
TO THE MALL?: A PARENT'S GUIDE TO THE NEW TEENAGER
Anthony E. Wolf, Ph.D.

THE GOOD SON: SHAPING THE MORAL DEVELOPMENT
OF OUR BOYS AND YOUNG MEN
Michael Gurian

THE HEALTHY YOUNG CHILD
Sari F. Edelstein

INFANTS AND MOTHERS: DIFFERENCES IN DEVELOPMENT
T. Berry Brazelton, M.D.

KIDS ARE WORTH IT: GIVING YOUR CHILD THE GIFT OF INNER DISCIPLINE
Barbara Coloroso

KNOW YOUR CHILD: THE AUTHORITATIVE GUIDE FOR TODAY'S PARENTS
Stella Chess, M.D. and Alexander Thomas, M.D.

LATE BLOOMERS
Brendan Gill

LEARNED OPTIMISM: HOW TO CHANGE YOUR MIND AND YOUR LIFE
Martin E. P. Seligman, Ph.D.

STOP STRUGGLING WITH YOUR CHILD: QUICK-TIP PARENTING
SOLUTIONS THAT WILL WORK FOR YOU—AND YOUR KIDS AGES 4 TO 12
Evonne Weinhaus and Karen Friedman

STOP STRUGGLING WITH YOUR TEEN
Evonne Weinhaus and Karen Friedman

STUDY POWER : STUDY SKILLS TO IMPROVE YOUR LEARNING
AND YOUR GRADES
William R. Luckie, Ph.D. and Wood Smethurst

TEACHING A YOUNG CHILD TO READ
Wood Smethurst

TEACHING AND JOY
Edited by Robert Sornson and James Scott

TEACHING IN THE KEY OF LIFE
Mimi Brodsky Chenfeld

TEACHING YOUR CHILD THE LANGUAGE OF SOCIAL SUCCESS
(and other books by the authors) *Marshall P. Duke, Ph.D., Stephen Nowicki Jr., Ph.D., and Elisabeth A. Martin, M.Ed.*

36 CHILDREN
Herbert Kohl

THE WATER IS WIDE
Pat Conroy

WHAT TEENS NEED TO SUCCEED: PROVEN, PRACTICAL WAYS TO SHAPE
YOUR OWN FUTURE
Peter L. Benson, Ph.D., Judy Galbraith, M.A., and Pamela Espeland

WHAT TO EXPECT THE FIRST YEAR
Arlene Eisenberg, Heidi E. Murkoff, and Sandee E. Hathaway

WHY YOUR CHILD IS HYPERACTIVE
Ben F. Feingold, M.D.

243

WINNING CHILDREN OVER
Francis X. Walton and Robert Powers

WINNING TEENAGERS OVER IN HOME AND SCHOOL : A MANUAL FOR
PARENTS, TEACHERS, COUNSELORS, AND PRINCIPALS
Francis X. Walton

WISDOM OF THE JEWISH SAGES: A MODERN READING OF PIRKE AVOT
Rami M. Shapiro

WITHOUT SPANKING OR SPOILING: A PRACTICAL APPROACH
TO TODDLER AND PRESCHOOL GUIDANCE
Elizabeth Crary

THE WONDER OF BOYS: WHAT PARENTS, MENTORS AND EDUCATORS CAN
DO TO SHAPE BOYS INTO EXCEPTIONAL MEN
Michael Gurian

CHILDREN'S BOOKS

ALWAYS MY DAD
Written by Sharon Dennis Wyeth and illustrated by Raul Colon

AND THEN WHAT HAPPENED, PAUL REVERE? (and other books by the author)
Written by Jean Fritz and illustrated by Margot Tomes

THE BEGINNER'S BIBLE: TIMELESS CHILDREN'S STORIES
Karyn Henley

BREAD AND JAM FOR FRANCES
Written by Russell Hoban and illustrated by Lillian Hoban

THE CAT IN THE HAT
Written and illustrated by Dr. Seuss

CHARLOTTE'S WEB
Written by E. B. White

CITY: A STORY OF ROMAN PLANNING AND CONSTRUCTION
(and other books by the author) *Written and illustrated by David MacAulay*

THE COMPLETE TALES OF WINNIE-THE-POOH
Written by A. A. Milne and illustrated by Ernest H. Shepard

DINNER AT AUNT CONNIE'S HOUSE
Written and illustrated by Faith Ringgold

FLOWER GARDEN
Written by Eve Bunting and illustrated by Kathryn Hewitt

FLY AWAY HOME
Written by Eve Bunting and illustrated by Ronald Himler

FROG AND TOAD ARE FRIENDS
Written and illustrated by Arnold Lobel

THE GARDENER
Written by Sarah Stewart and illustrated by David Small

HARRY POTTER AND THE SORCERER'S STONE (and other books by the author)
Written by J. K. Rowling

THE KISSING HAND
Written by Audrey Penn and illustrated by Ruth E. Harper and Nancy M. Leak

THE LITTLE ENGINE THAT COULD
Written by Watty Piper and illustrated by George Hauman

THE LOST LAKE
Written and illustrated by Allen Say

LOVE YOU FOREVER
Written by Robert Munsch and illustrated by Sheila McGraw

MIKE MULLIGAN AND HIS STEAM SHOVEL
Written and illustrated by Virginia Lee Burton

THE NEW TAKE JOY
Written and illustrated by Tasha Tudor

OH, THE PLACES YOU'LL GO!
Written and illustrated by Dr. Seuss

ONCE UPON A POTTY
Written and illustrated by Alona Frankel

OUR GRANNY
Written by Margaret Wild and illustrated by Julie Vivas

THE REAL MOTHER GOOSE
Illustrated by Blanche Fisher Wright

THE SNOWY DAY
Written and illustrated by Ezra Jack Keats

SOMETHING FROM NOTHING
Written and illustrated by Phoebe Gilman

THE STORY OF FERDINAND
Written by Munro Leaf and illustrated by Robert Lawson

THE TRUMPET OF THE SWAN
Written by E. B. White and illustrated by Edward Frascino

TUCKING MOMMY IN
Written by Morag Loh and illustrated by Donna Rawlins

THE TWO OF THEM
Written and illustrated by Aliki

UNCLE JED'S BARBER SHOP
Written by Margaree King Mitchell and illustrated by James Ransome

WHAT YOU KNOW FIRST
Written by Patricia MacLachlan and illustrated by Barry Moser

WHERE THE SIDEWALK ENDS: THE POEMS AND DRAWINGS
OF SHEL SILVERSTEIN
Written and illustrated by Shel Silverstein

*WHERE THE WILD THINGS ARE
Written and illustrated by Maurice Sendak

WILFRID GORDON MCDONALD PARTRIDGE
Written by Mem Fox and illustrated by Julie Vivas

245

About the Editors

Marshall P. Duke, Ph.D., is currently Charles Howard Candler Professor of Psychology at Emory University. During his three decades at Emory, he has served as director of the University Counseling Center and chair of the Department of Psychology and has won numerous teaching awards. In addition to working clinically with children for over thirty years, he has been a consultant for public and private schools throughout the U.S. and Great Britain. With Dr. Stephen Nowicki, he is coauthor of a textbook on abnormal psychology and two books dealing with social problems in children, HELPING THE CHILD WHO DOESN'T FIT IN and TEACHING YOUR CHILD THE LANGUAGE OF SOCIAL SUCCESS. Dr. Duke's work has been written about in myriad publications, including the *New York Times,* the *Boston Globe, Newsweek,* and *Parents* magazine. Among his numerous broadcast appearances are National Public Radio's *Parents Journal, The Today Show,* and *The Oprah Winfrey Show.* With his coeditor and partner for thirty-six years, he has three children and five grandchildren.

Sara Bookman Duke, a native of New Jersey, has lived in Atlanta for over thirty years. She graduated from Indiana University in 1964 with a major in history. She returned to graduate training in 1977 and received her master's degree in medical science (M.M.Sc.) in communicative disorders and learning disabilities from the Emory University School of Medicine in 1979. Early in her career, she worked at Atlanta's highly regarded Howard School for children with special needs. In 1987, Sara entered into private practice as an educational consultant primarily involved in diagnostics, individualized program development, and identification of optimal school placements. In her long career, Sara has worked with more than 2500 children, giving her a level of experience shared by few others in her field. As such, she is a popular speaker before parent groups and is among the most respected professionals in the Atlanta area. Sara and her coeditor (and husband) have three children and five grandchildren.